MEDIA, FEMINISM, CULTURAL STUDIES

The Sacred Cinema of Andrei Tarkovsky
by Jeremy Mark Robinson

Liv Tyler
by Thomas A. Christie

The Cinema of Hayao Miyazaki
Jeremy Mark Robinson

Stepping Forward: Essays, Lectures and Interviews
by Wolfgang Iser

The Christmas Movie Book
by Thomas A. Christie

Wild Zones: Pornography, Art and Feminism
by Kelly Ives

'Cosmo Woman': The World of Women's Magazines
by Oliver Whitehorne

The Cinema of Richard Linklater
by Thomas A. Christie

Andrea Dworkin
by Jeremy Mark Robinson

Cixous, Irigaray, Kristeva: The Jouissance of French Feminism
by Kelly Ives

The Erotic Object: Sexuality in Sculpture From Prehistory to the Present Day
by Susan Quinnell

Women in Pop Music
by Helen Challis

Sex in Art: Pornography and Pleasure in Painting and Sculpture
by Cassidy Hughes

Erotic Art
by Cassidy Hughes

John Hughes
by Thomas A. Christie

Jean-Luc Godard: The Passion of Cinema / Le Passion de Cinéma
by Jeremy Mark Robinson

Genius and Loving It! Mel Brooks
by Thomas Christie

The Comic Art of Mel Brooks
by Maurice Yacowar

Marvelous Names
by P. Adams Sitney

The Art of Katsuhiro Otomo
by Jeremy Mark Robinson

Akira: The Movie and the Manga
by Jeremy Mark Robinson

The Art of Masamune Shirow (3 vols)
by Jeremy Mark Robinson

Detonation Britain: Nuclear War in the UK
by Jeremy Mark Robinson

Julia Kristeva: Art, Love, Melancholy, Philosophy, Semiotics
by Kelly Ives

Luce Irigaray: Lips, Kissing, and the Politics of Sexual Difference
by Kelly Ives

Helene Cixous I Love You: The Jouissance *of Writing*
by Kelly Ives

FORTHCOMING BOOKS

Legend of the Overfiend
Death Note
Naruto
Bleach
Hellsing
Vampire Knight
Mushishi
One Piece
Nausicaä of the Valley of the Wind
Tsui Hark

The Ecstatic Cinema of Tony Ching Siu-tung
The Twilight Saga
Jackie Collins and the Blockbuster Novel
Harry Potter

IMMORAL TALES

Immoral Tales

Walerian Borowczyk

POCKET MOVIE GUIDE

Jeremy Mark Robinson

CRESCENT MOON

First published 2022.
© Jeremy Mark Robinson 2022.

Set in Rotis Serif 9 on 12pt, and Gill Sans Light display.
Designed by Radiance Graphics.

British Library Cataloguing in Publication data available for this title.

ISBN-13 9781861718563

Crescent Moon Publishing
P.O. Box 1312
Maidstone, Kent
ME14 5XU, Great Britain
www.crmoon.com

CONTENTS

ACKNOWLEDGEMENTS

To the copyright holders of the illustrations.
To authors quoted and their publishers.

PICTURE CREDITS

Argos Films. Pagan. Cult Epics. Severin Films. Naja Films. Palace Video. New Horizon. Gaumont/ Columbia. C.A.V. Distribution. Nouveaux Pictures. Arrow. New Line Cinema. Sara Distribution. Jupiter Communications. C.D.F. Films. Lisa Film. Top Video.

Omnia vincit Amor: et nos cedamus Amori.
Love carries all before him: we too must yield to Love.

Virgil, *Aenid* (X. 69)

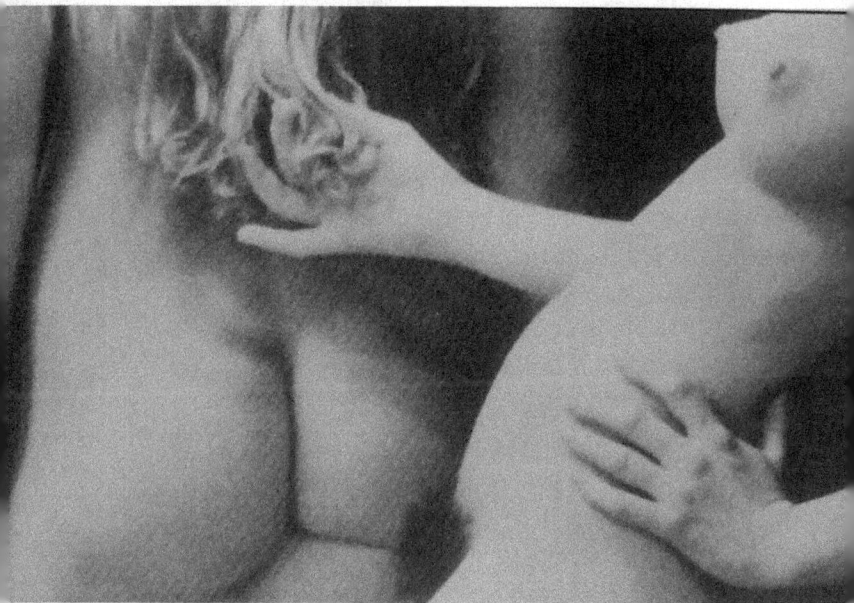

Walerian Borowczyk's Immoral Tales (1974)

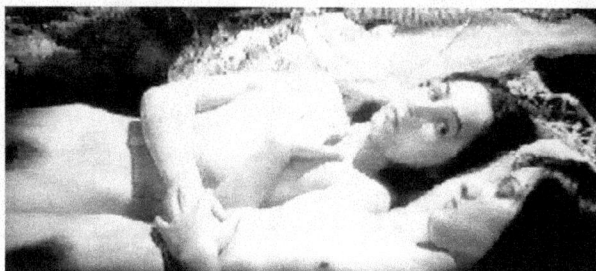

Prix de l'Âge d'Or

UNMORALISCHE
GESCHICHTEN

Film von
WALERIAN BOROWCZYK

mit
PALOMA PICASSO
LISE DANVERS FABRICE LUCHINI
CHARLOTTE ALEXANDRA
PASCALE CHRISTOPHE FLORENCE BELLAMY
© ARGOS FILMS

PART ONE

$*$

WALERIAN BOROWCZYK

I

THE CINEMA OF
WALERIAN BOROWCZYK

Eroticism, sex, is one of the most moral parts of life.
Eroticism does not kill, exterminate, encourage evil,
lead to crime. On the contrary, it makes people
gentler, brings joy, gives fulfilment, leads to selfless
pleasure.

Walerian Borowczyk[1]

1 Interview with Andrzej Markowski, *Kino*, 4, 1975.

Walerian Borowczyk (known as 'Boro') is one of cinema's one-offs. Quite simply, there is no filmmaker quite like Borowczyk. Borowczyk's movies have an extraordinary, magical quality. They reach a place very rare in contemporary cinema, and are quite unlike the pictures of any other filmmaker. Borowczyk's films create their own space, with imagery, sounds and music of a really exceptional power.

Goto: Island of Love was the first Walerian Borowczyk film that made a big impression on audiences and critics, winning a number of prizes. I first saw *Goto: Island of Love* in 1982, at Bournemouth Film School, when we watched 16mm prints as part of our film history course. You could see there was an astonishing vision at work here. I remember above all the creation of a visceral, idiosyncratic and original world.

If I had to single out some movies, I'd cite *Blanche, Immoral Tales, Behind Convent Walls, The Story of Sin, Angels' Games, The Beast* and *Goto*, for their painterly sense, the use of props and costumes, and the incredible attention to detail. Very sophisticated, mysterious, poetic. Not forgetting the acute awareness of the history of religion and literature. Walerian Borowczyk produced some of the most memorable images in European cinema, the equal of Ingmar Bergman, Sergei Paradjanov or Andrei Tarkovsky. (Yet, it's the stories and the characters, the movement and the drama that Borowczyk himself enshrines, not pretty images).

I reckon there's one absolute Walerian Borowczyk masterpiece, and that's *Goto: Island of Love*. That can rank alongside the great films in the history of cinema. I'd put *Immoral Tales* in the masterpiece class too (*Blanche* is rated also very highly by many critics).[2] The other Borowczyk films are often as fascinating, often more grotesque – certainly more sexually explicit – but probably not as wholly satisfying as *Goto: Island of Love* – from a conventional, film critical standpoint. But *The Beast, Blanche, Behind Convent Walls*, and *Love Rites* would count as noteworthy items by most standards.[3] They may not be quite up there with *Persona* (Ingmar Bergman, 1966) or *8 1/2* (Federico Fellini, 1963) or *The Gospel According To Matthew* (Pier Paolo Pasolini,

2 Tho' *Blanche* doesn't reach as high in ambition as either *Goto* or *Immoral Tales*.
3 For detractors, Borowczyk's films were better when they concerned ideas rather than the senses – philosophy not sex.

1964),[4] but taken together they form a group of works that mark Borowczyk out as a maverick original.

Walerian Borowczyk isn't a filmmaker seen by the critical community as in the front rank. He's not celebrated like Akira Kurosawa, F.W. Murnau, Orson Welles, Tsui Hark, Jean Renoir or Sergei Eisenstein, and his films don't make critics' top ten lists. Why? Partly because only *Goto* is regarded as a genuine masterpiece, whereas Kurosawa, Tsui, Welles, Renoir, Murnau *et al* directed several masterworks (and some are the greatest movies ever made – *Citizen Kane, The Magnificent Ambersons, The Seven Samurai, Kagemusha, The Grand Illusion, Sunrise, The Last Laugh, Once Upon a Time In China*, etc). Partly because the other films helmed by Boro have been regarded as too obscure, too niche, too esoteric. Partly because Borowczyk seldom enjoyed significant financial success (*Immoral Tales* and *The Story of Sin* seem to have been Boro's only hit movies economically[5]). Partly because he generally avoided commercial subjects and big stars. Partly because Borowczyk wasn't a media darling (like Fellini, Welles or Tsui), and didn't play the publicity game.

Contemplating Walerian Borowczyk's lack of major status, one could point items such as: he avoided 'commercial' productions • the unavailability of key works (and the poor dubbed versions of others) • the timing was wrong • he fell out with producers • he didn't play the media game (like courting journalists) • he was too critical of authority • his films were too niche/ *avant garde* • the porn elements undermined his reputation • he didn't capitalize enough on the success of *Goto* • and critics are less amenable to Eastern European filmmakers than those from the West (altho' that didn't apply to Polanski, Wadja, Forman, etc).

---

4 The cinema of Walerian Borowczyk has many affinities with that of Pier Paolo Pasolini: both come from the same highly intellectual, highly educated, European backgrounds which valorize *avant garde* art, philosophy (Existentialism), Surrealism, de Sade, etc. Both were mavericks. Both produced controversial Euro-art movies which included plenty of eroticism and nudity as well as politically provocative subject matter.
5 And *The Story of Sin* only in Poland.

You probably won't know many people who've even heard of Walerian Borowczyk, let alone seen one of his films. His reputation as a producer of European arty/ porny films (art-as-porn films or porn-as-art films), is probably all that many people will have heard of him (movies with sex and nudity do seem to travel well, as film producers and distributors know), but likely they won't have seen them. Needless to say, Borowczyk's films are *not* shown regularly on television,[6] even by TV channels (including cable and satellite services) which boast of their open-mindedness and international film broadcasts.[7]

Similarly, you won't see Walerian Borowczyk's pictures at the cinema nowadays; even rep and arthouse and independent cinemas rarely screen his films. It's mainly home video releases (and, later, home DVD/ Blu-ray releases) that's enabled Borowczyk's films to reach a contemporary audience (the porny and arty elements make them perfect for niche marketing to the cognoscenti). And you'll have to hunt to find them all. You won't find *The Beast* next to *Back To the Future* and *Bad Boys* on the 'B' shelf in your local video store.

Several of Borowczyk's films as director are *not* out in the world in the form that the director preferred. Boro suffered meddling producers, material being added to and cut from his movies, his films were re-titled, and so on. It's a sad tale that is found everywhere in the commercial film industry, even for important filmmakers.

It's frustrating that so many of Borowczyk's 14 feature-length films (13 live action movies plus one animated film) are still hard to find in some regions of this amazing planet. Especially when there's so much other dreck readily available.[8] (Thousands of completely worthless movies are available everywhere, yet thousands of gems still languish in vaults, or are subject to copyright/ ownership disputes, or have vanished. There

6 In Great Britain at least.
7 I can think of maybe one occasion when *Goto: Island of Love* was shown in Britain in 25 years, but I may be wrong about that.
8 You can see some of Borowczyk's short films on the excellent UbuWeb Film site (ubu.com), and also YouTube (youtube.com).

are many well-known lost films).

Even the ten or so films available in the U.S.A. and Britain are difficult to track down – you'll have to try the usual places – Amazon, E-bay, etc – but there'll be plenty more hunting around to find the rarer items.

I found *The Art of Love* from a distributor in Athens, Greece (New Star), *Three Immoral Women* from a video outlet in New Jersey (DVD Legacy), and *Emmanuelle 5* from a seller on Amazon (Vinyl Exchange, Manchester, GB).

Another problem with assessing Boro's work is the quality of the prints, DVDs and videos available – this is a fantastically visual filmmaker, but some prints are so washed-out and nasty. Then there's the aspect of the sound and dubbing: some Borowczyk movies are only available in dubbed versions, rather than the much-preferred original soundtrack plus subtitles (dubbed versions probably won't have been overseen by Borowczyk – in which case they can't be regarded as 'directed by' Borowczyk. Some English dubs (I mean, *American English* dubs)[9] of Borowczyk's films are workman-like and some are terrible. Dubbed versions, as we know, alter 100s of elements of a movie, not only the dialogue/ language. The sound mixes, for instance, such a crucial aspect of Boro's cinema, are changed in dubbed films. Different music is attached; music is cut. The original filmmakers do *not* usually record and mix the overseas dubs of their movies. However, Jean-Luc Godard preferred dubbed versions of his own films – they were more honest, he reckoned).

However, for a time Walerian Borowczyk's films were popular, or at least they were on general release in theatres. According to David Cook's *A History of Narrative Film* (one of the best books on cinema ever, a total must-have), *The Story of Sin* was the most popular film in Poland in 1975, and *Immoral Tales* was the second most successful film in the erotic sector in France in 1974, behind *Emmanuelle* (that means a *lot* of people

9 Why aren't there Australian English dubs? Or Indian English dubs? (Yes, I know why).

saw it – the French love movies more than almost anyone in the world. According to the magazine *Le Film francaise*, 359,748 tickets were sold for *Immoral Tales*).[10]

Immoral Tales was crucial for Walerian Borowczyk's cinema: it was a renowned, European film producer (Anatole Dauman) offering him a gig. And his first three features – *Kabal, Goto* and *Blanche* – hadn't set the box office on fire. A hit movie makes everyone take notice in the ferociously competitive, cutthroat world of commercial cinema. Producer Dauman would say, let's do it again, and Borowczyk seemed to happy to go for it, too. Thus, the financial impact of *Immoral Tales* certainly encouraged a move towards further erotic movies in Boro's career – to *The Beast,* to *Behind Convent Walls*, to *Three Immoral Women*, etc (plus beefing up the erotic content in *The Story of Sin*).

They *are* an acquired taste, but once you've seen a Walerian Borowczyk film, you don't forget it. No one else makes movies quite like Borowczyk's; the word 'unique' is thrown around a lot in critical circles, about this or that writer, this or that actor, this or that painter. But Borowczyk's films truly are unique. As soon as that classical organ music starts up, completely distinctive, you know you're entering Borowczyk Land, a very strange place. Music's a big part of the Borowczyk world: you won't hear music like this anywhere else in cinema – and certainly not in *these* contexts. Again, many filmmakers are cited as having a distinctive way of using music – Shoji Kawamori, Martin Scorsese, Stanley Kubrick, Robert Altman, etc – but Borowczyk's music has carved out its own niche. I must stop using the word 'unique' to describe Borowczyk's cinema, but he really is a man of unique talents.

Borowczyk's cinema is a blink-and-you-miss-it type, a cinema where you think, 'wait, did I see that?' It's a combination of the eccentric editing style and the even more eccentric storytelling. It's striking, for ex, how many critics and fans disagree about what they saw in

---

10 C. Tohill, 55. Cinema admissions in 1973 were 176 million, down from 276 million in 1964.

Borowczyk's films. This occasionally crops up in film criticism – even respected critics will claim that something occurred when it didn't. But they thought it did.

Walerian Borowczyk, of course, is an accomplished magician of sleight of hand. Cinema is all trickery. *All* of it (often it's at its most fake when it appears to be its most 'real' or 'realistic'). And Borowczyk's films are very clever at persuading the audience to get into a suitable state of mind for sleights of hand to become invisible.

You probably won't recognize many of the performers in Walerian Borowczyk's films. He didn't use big stars well-known in the West, except once: Sylvia Kristel, darling of the Euro art film/ porn scene in the mid-1970s. There are some recognizable actors in some of Borowczyk's films, though: Patrick Magee, Udo Keir, and Joe Dallesandro (one of the very few Americans in Boro's casts), and for a European audience, Michel Simon and Pierre Brasseur will be very familiar (especially in La France). But everyone else in Borowczyk's cinema is nearly all French or Italian, and they're actors you've probably never seen before (or since).[11]

You might recognize Massimo Girotti and Laura Betti (from *The Art of Love*) from the movies of Pier Paolo Pasolini, and Pablo Picasso's daughter Paloma appeared in her only film role in *Immortal Tales*.

Walerian Borowczyk was sometimes denigrated for being too obsessed with style, with the look – he was called a Mannerist, a Baroque artist. The same accusations have been made of Pier Paolo Pasolini, Bernardo Bertolucci, Stanley Kubrick and Peter Greenaway (yes, even film critics – God bless them! – don't know their art history as well as they should when referring to the Baroque or Mannerist eras).[12]

Walerian Borowczyk's films are completely un-politically correct. But you probably already knew that. It's not that Borowczyk sets out to offend (although there is something of the trickster, the Surrealist/ *avant garde*

11 With the odd German, Scandinavian or Brit.
12 The Mannerist artists – Pomtormo, Michelangelo, Rosso – were some of Boro's favourites.

épater of the bourgeoisie about Borowczyk, as with many artists).[13] Rather, Borowczyk simply puts in his films what he wants (or he seems to – of course, there were run-ins with producers, censors, distributors, etc, as for any professional film director working in the commercial sector. Anatole Dauman gave him a free hand, but other producers didn't).

⚜

It's a delight to be able to see more of Borowczyk's work in decent quality releases in recent years. Really, everything by Boro should be released in the best available versions. (An ideal that should extend to all of the great filmmakers, but it just doesn't happen. It's disheartening how many important works are not available to see).

We could explore many theoretical aspects of the cinema of Walerian Borowczyk; I have suggested some approaches. But Borowczyk's films openly deconstruct themselves before our eyes. There's no need to analyze Borowczyk's works from, say, a Freudian perspective, because the works have already done that. At the very least, a Freudian, psychoanalytical deconstruction of the movie and the plot is always included in a Borowczyk piece. (In a similar way, the best spoof of *Star Wars* would be to show... *Star Wars*).

WALERIAN BOROWCZYK: BIOGRAPHY

Born on September 2, 1923 in Kwilcz in Poland, Walerian Borowczyk died on February 3, 2006 in Paris. He married Ligia Brokowska in 1950. Borowczyk studied at the Cracow Academy of Fine Arts from 1946 (Andrzej

---

13 Jean-Luc Godard and Pier Paolo Pasolini come to mind. The aim of shocking the bourgeoisie (that childish goal of too many leftist/ Marxist artists), may derive in part from the attempt at reaching a realm where the bourgeoisie and their ideals do not go. That is, to go beyond the limits of what is accepted by bourgeois society, into the crude, the ultra-violent, the bestial.

Wajda[14] was a fellow student), as a painter. The Republic of Poland has a population of 38 million (in 1997), and a land mass of 120,728 square miles. The State-run film school in Poland, the Leon Schille State Film School in Lodz, was founded in 1948. Four-fifths of directors in Poland were trained there (tho' not Borowczyk). Other well-known Polish filmmakers include: Andrzej Munk, Jerzy Skolimowski, Krzystzof Zanussi, Roman Polanski, Agnieszka Holland and Krzysztof Kieslowski. Popular Polish animators of Borowczyk's era included: Jan Lenica, Daniel Szczechura, Zbig Rybczinski, Piotr Dumala, Witold Giersz, Zitman, Janik, Kotowski, Daniel Szczechura, and Wladyslaw Nehrebecki.

Walerian Borowczyk wrote (or co-wrote) as well as directed most of his films; that's a very important point: it means that Borowczyk was much closer to being the true 'author' of his films than directors for hire (even the most celebrated directors *do not* write their own movies). It also means that Borowczyk was sometimes the *originator* of his films: they didn't come from some outside influence or source, like a film producer or a studio.

For several years in the early 1960s, Walerian Borowczyk worked for Les Cinéastes Associés, an animation company run by millionaire entrepreneur Jacques Forgeot (he joined in 1959). Cinéastes Associés was very large for an animation house in Europe in the 1960s, with some 70 employees (its star animators included Alexander Alexeieff, Etienne Raik and the Bettiol brothers). Borowczyk took advantage of the resources to create his animated short films and TV commercials (however, he had a maverick status within the firm; Borowczyk was not a company man, a regular employee who fitted in). Many elements that appeared in Borowczyk's later live-action movies were developed at Cinéastes Associés. (Borowczyk left Cinéastes Associés to

14 The 'Polish School' of filmmakers developed between 1954 and 1963; it included Andrzej Wajda, Andrzej Munk, and Wojciech Has. (The 'Polish School' flourished during the Soviet thaw of the 1950s: Poland has had two periods of liberalization: 1954-1963 and 1976-1981).

start his own company, Pantaleon Films, with one of his regular collaborators, Dominique Duvergé).

Based in the City of Light for much of his life, after moving there from Poland[15] in 1958,[16] when he was 35, Walerian Borowczyk was a painter and illustrator who went on to create short animated films (which included *Holy Smoke* (1963), *Angels' Games* (1964), and *Joachim's Dictionary* (1965)). One of the first visits to Paris for Borowczyk was in 1954, to make a film about the artist Fernand Léger (*The Studio of Fernand Léger*,1954). Polish artists and intellectuals had gravitated towards Paris for centuries (since 1795, Poland had been partitioned between Russia, Austria and Prussia). As Friedrich Nietzsche put it in *Ecce Homo:* 'an artist, a man has no home in Europe save in Paris'.

The chance to work on a wider range of subjects would be one of the appeals of working in the West for Borowczyk – in Poland, as in the rest of Eastern Europe, censorship places limitations on topics (whether imposed by the State, Communist agencies, or artistic and social conformism). Certainly Boro's film career would not be the same had he stayed in Warsaw (censorship directly affected the films and careers of fellow Poles such as Andrzej Wadja, Jerry Skolimowski, Ryszard Bugajski, Aleksander Ford, and Janusz Zaorski).

And there was more money available for film production in France than in Poland. According to David Cook in *A History of Narrative Film*, the Polish film industry in the 1980s operated on a low budget: film stock was hard to come by, so that going for more than two takes was seldom allowed, actors often worked on several films at the same time to make a living (as also in the Hong Kong film industry), and productions were turned around in 30 days because equipment was so scarce. Yet the film industry in Poland employed 30,000 people.

---

15 Many Polish filmmakers went into exile, along with 100s of others in the Eastern Bloc countries. The Warsaw Pact was formalized in 1955.
16 Roman Polanski is the best-known Polish filmmaker who ended up in Paris.

If Boro had stayed in East Europe, and worked in the Polish film industry, it would mean being part of the centralized, State-run, socialist industry, with the government administering the whole film business, from production to distribution (the State owned or ran film distributors, theatres, etc, with the Minister of Culture presiding over film production, and controlling all financing). Boro returned to Poland to direct *The Story of Sin*, but that was the only time he made a feature-length production in his home country.

Many of Borowczyk's first animations were made with Jan Lenica (1928-2001),[17] mainly in the late Fifties: *Dom, Love Requited, Banner of Youth,* and *Once There Was.* (Borowczyk directed 22 short films before his move into features with *Goto, Island of Love* in 1969, and 8 short films afterwards[18]).

Prior to 1989, most animation in East Europe was paid for and distributed by State-run film studios, such as SeMaFor and Experimental Cartoon Film Studio in Poland, Kratky Film in the Czech Republic and AnimaFilm in Romania. In Poland, the animation house Experimental Cartoon Film Studio was central – it was established in 1947 (in Katowice – later it moved to Bielsko Biala in 1956).

The key film organization in Poland was the production house Film Polski, founded in 1945 (when the film industry was nationalized). Like other institutions in Communist nations, it was split into individual production units (*zespol*), the United Groups of Film Producers, run by filmmakers (typically, the units were run by a film director, an executive producer and a literary manager, with usually younger filmmakers working under them). In 1980 there were 8 film units, each operating for a three-year period. 1956 had been an important year – when Gomulka came to power, and five film units were established (Andrez Wajda identifies this as the real start of the Polish School in cinema). Polski Film had 4 chief studios: Cracow, Lodz, Wroclaw and

17 Lenica emigrated to Paris in 1963.
18 Source: Internet Movie Database.

W.D.F.I.F. in the capital.

Other early Borowczyk films (some only seconds long) included: *School* (1958), *House* (1958), *The Astronauts* (1959), *The Concert of Mr and Mrs Kabal* (1962), *Renaissance* (1963), *The Encyclopedia of Grandmother* (1963), *Rosalie* (1966), *Diptych* (1967) and *Gavotte* (1967). In his animations, Walerian Borowczyk employed a variety of techniques, including pixillation, stop-motion, loops, collage, cel animation and painting on the film itself. Many of the techniques were either easy to produce (pixillation) or cheap (repetition, reycling and other effects achieved with editing).

This is filmmaking as magic, very much in the manner of the work of Géorges Méliès, where trick photography, special effects and the mechanics of cinema are celebrated as things in themselves. It is self-conscious cinema, cinema always aware of itself as cinema – a thing, an object, a machine, a technology, a process, a colour, a movement.

Storytelling and characters are thus only one aspect of many in Boro's cinema: his work enshrines the plasticity of the image, the feeling of celluloid running thru a camera, an editing machine or a film projector, the physicality of light (even digital animation or computer aided imagery is light), and the eternally fascinating mystery of objects and props (in the Surrealist manner).

Most of Walerian Borowczyk's feature films were made in French, and in France. He also shot in Italy, Germany, Sweden and Poland. He was Polish, and spoke French as a second language (but not much English): the French aspect of Boro's cinema gives it a particular cultural inflection. And yet not a hybrid: Boro's work remains resolutely, stubbornly Eastern European (look at the short animations – the sensibility is East European, not French).

Let's not forget that France has one of the strongest film cultures in the world: France produces more films than any country in Europe, and people go to the cinema more times a year in France than anywhere else in Europa. More European co-productions are made with

French companies than any other country. In short, France is a very good place to make films.

(And Paris in the 1950s and 1960s, when Boro moved there, was one of the best places in the world to *see* films (and it still is). Apart from Henri Langlois' Cinémathèque, one of the central cultural and social platforms of the whole New Wave, there were many ciné-clubs and specialist cinemas. The French *cinéphiles,* like Jean-Luc Godard, Francois Truffaut and Eric Rohmer, seemed to spend whole days and weeks watching movies. With his fellow cinéastes Truffaut and Rivette, Godard would regularly watch 3 or 4 movies a day. Godard and Rivette, for instance, saw *Macbeth* (Orson Welles, 1948) repeatedly from 2 p.m. to 10 p.m. They haunted the famous Cinémathèque, as well as the C.C.Q.L.)

❀

The thirteen features directed by Walerian Borowczyk are:

> *Mr. and Mrs. Kabal's Theatre* (1967)
> *Goto, Island of Love* (1969)
> *Blanche* (1972)
> *Immoral Tales* (1974)
> *The Story of Sin* (1975)
> *The Beast* (1975)
> *The Streetwalker* (1976)
> *Behind Convent Walls* (1978)
> *Three Immoral Women* (1979)
> *The Strange Case of Doctor Jeckyll and Miss Osbourne* (1981)
> *The Art of Love* (1983)
> *Emmanuelle 5* (1987)
> *Love Rites* (1987)
> Plus the TV film *Lulu* (1980)

Walerian Borowczyk's first feature film in live-action was the singular *Goto: Island of Love* (1969), although a feature of his collected animation was released before that: *The Théatre of Mr and Mrs Kabal* (1967). *Goto: Island of Love* was followed by *The*

Phonograph (1969), *Blanche* (1972), *A Private Collection* (1973), *Contes Immoraux* (*Immoral Tales,* 1974) and *Histoire d'un Péché* (*The Story of Sin,* 1975).

La Bête (*The Beast,* 1975) was Walerian Borowczyk's most controversial film, a mixture of French farce, surrealism, and a lot of sex (including bestiality). Borowczyk's next film, *La Marge* (1976, *The Margin,* a.k.a. *The Streetwalker* and *Emmanuelle '77*), again combined eroticism, Existentialism and Surrealism; it was based on Borowczyk's friend André Pieyre de Mandiargues' 1967 novel, and starred Sylvia Kristel (of the *Emmanuelle* films) and Joe Dallesandro (of Andy Warhol's coterie).

Other films followed, including: *Letter From Paris* (1975, for German TV), *Interieur d'un Convent* (*Behind Convent Walls,* 1978), *Belt of Fire* (1978), about the mass murderer Gilles de Rais, *Les Héroïnes du Mal* (*Three Immoral Women,* 1979), *L'Armoire* (*The Wardrobe,* part of the *Private Collections* anthology feature, 1979), *Lulu* (1980), taken from Franz Wedekind's two *Lulu* plays, which have been adapted several times,[19] *The Strange Case of Dr Jeckyll and Miss Osbourne* (a.k.a. *Blood of Dr Jeckyll/ The Experiment,* 1981), *Ars Amandi* (*The Art of Love,* 1983), based on Ovid, four episodes of *Série Rose* (1986-1991), a cable TV series, and 1987's *Cérémonie d'Amour* (a.k.a. *Love Rites*).[20]

Many of these European art films contained Walerian Borowczyk's trademarks – surrealism, sex, violence, political satire, hyper-intricate art direction, bizarre incidents, unusual music, all seen thru Borowczyk's unique, Freudian/ Surrealist vision.

Some of Borowczyk's movies were based on existing properties – novels (*Blanche, The Story of Sin, The Strange Case of Dr. Jeckyll and Miss Osbourne,* the *Série Rose* shows and *Behind Convent Walls*), plays (*Lulu*),

---

19 They formed the basis of *Pandora's Box,* G.W. Pabst, 1928 – it was brave of Boro to take on a movie regarded as a classic.
20 *Love Rites,* Boro's final feature, starred Mathieu Carrière as a man who meets a prostitute (Marina Pierro) on the Paris Métro. Pierro, who had appeared in *The Art of Love* and *Dr Jeckyll,* was superb as the mysterious, eternal prostitute, a mythical figure recalling the 'holy whores' of ancient religions.

stories (*Immoral Tales, Three Immoral Women, La Marge, The Art of Love, Love Rites*), and some were originals: *Kabal, The Beast* and *Goto* (most of Borowczyk's short films were original works). Some were remakes (*Dr Jeckyll* and *Lulu*). Some were sequels (*Three Immoral Women*, a sequel, in form and content, anyway, to *Immoral Tales*). And some were part of movie franchises (*Emmanuelle 5*).

So Walerian Borowczyk was no different from most film directors in drawing on short stories, novels and plays for the bulk of his feature work. Which contradicts the received view of Boro as an *auteur* who comes up with *everything*, including the concepts, the characters and the stories for his films.

In 1986, Borowczyk made *Emmanuelle 5*, which seemed to confirm his softcore porn status for detractors. *Emmanuelle 5* is the utterly embarrassing piece of shit in Walerian Borowczyk's *œuvre*, a shockingly inept film that even diehard fans and critics find impossible to explain away. In tackling the *Emmanuelle* franchise, though, Borowczyk sent it up (there was a scene set at the Cannes Film Festival, with audiences clamouring to see a fictional porn film, *Love Express*). But the lame satire wasn't enough to save *Emmanuelle 5*.

Notice, dear *cinéastes*, that recent retrospectives of Boro, such as at the Pompidou Centre in Paris in 2017, and organizations such as the Friends of Walerian Borowczyk, do not include *Emmanuelle 5* among Boro's works.[21] It seems like they're trying to pretend that it never happened.

But it did.

I too wish *Emmanuelle 5* didn't exist. But Borowczyk *did* direct parts of *Emmanuelle 5*, he *is* noted as writer/ co-writer, the film *is* part of Boro's official credits, and he *does* have the most sacred film credit of all for *Emmanuelle 5*: 'un film de' (however, 'un film de' is the stupidest credit in movies).

---

21 Nor the *Série Rose* TV series, and not *Lulu*, either. There may have been rights issues. However, the 2017 retrospective included little-known Borowczyk films such as *The Wardrobe* from *Private Collections* (1979).

The first joke in *The Naked Gun 2.5* (1991), the wonderful Zucker-Abrahams-Zucker movie, is a caption gag: 'Un Film de David Zucker' sends up the pretentious, irritating *auteur* credit that 99% of film directors *do not* deserve. Akira Kurosawa and Ingmar Bergman can legitimately use the 'a film by' credit (though they don't), but not Joe Nobody who's only directed one movie before and a couple of episodes of a rubbish TV drama[22]

The *auteur* credit, the 'un film de' credit, is dishonest and dumb. To be really accurate, 'a film by' should read, for *Immoral Tales* (1974): A film by Lise Danvers, Fabrice Luchini, Charlotte Alexandra, Florence Bellamy, Jacopo Berinizi, G. Lorenzo Berinizi, Pascale Christophe, Marie Forså, Paloma Picasso, Philippe Desboeuf, Robert Capia, Kjell Gustavsson, Tomas Hnevsa, Nicole Karen, Mathieu Rivollier, Gerard Tcherka, Anatole Dauman, Walerian Borowczyk, André Pieyre de Mandiargues, Maurice Le Roux, Bernard Daillencourt, Guy Durban, Noël Véry, Michel Zolat, Anne-Marie Sachs, Piet Bolscher, Dominique Duvergé, Alain Cayrade, Bernard Grignon, Maxine Groffsky, Alain Herpe, Jean-Pierre Platel and many others.

Who built the sets? Who booked the hotels? Who drew up all of the contracts (sometimes thousands for big movies)? Who oversaw the insurance, taxes, and liabilities? Who bought the cloth for the costumes? Who carried the lights up ten flights of stairs?[23] Who drove the actors to the locations? Who created the opticals for the titles? Who rented the vehicles? Who logged all of the rushes and takes? Who physically processed the exposed celluloid?

Not the director.[24]

This is a simplistic argument of who does what in movies, but *auteur* theory has also been denigrated on

22 Producer Budd Schulberg called the *auteur* theory 'one of the most overworked theories of all the theories that have come down about film'; the *auteur* theory only has real validity, Schulberg reckoned, 'when the director is also the writer of the screenplay' (in D. Georgakas & L. Rubenstein, eds. *Art Politics Cinema: The Cineaste Interviews*, Pluto Press, London, 1985, 364).
23 No elevators in some of those old buildings.
24 I could go on to list the 100s of jobs in movie production.

ideological, political, social and cultural grounds.

Anyway, how can *Emmanuelle 5* be 'un film de' when it's part of a franchise, when Boro *didn't* originate the project, when he *didn't* create the characters or the situations, when the director was hired by producers to make it, when he didn't agree with the casting (and when he didn't cast it), when it was co-written with others, when it was co-directed with others, and when it was edited, mixed and completed by others?

The Friends of Borowczyk and the 2017 Borowczyk retrospective in Paris also erased *The Art of Love* and the *Softly From Paris* TV series. According to the timeline and CV published by the Friends of Borowczyk, the *maître* directed the *Dr Jeckyll* adaptation in 1981, produced his last short animation in 1984 (*Scherzo Infernal*), finishing his feature career with *Love Rites* in 1987. So *The Art of Love,* the *Emmanuelle* sequel and the *Série Rose* TV series never happened.[25]

But they did.

Many *Star Wars* fans wish that *The Phantom Menace* (1999) had never occurred. But it did – that was a story that George Lucas wanted to tell, Jar-Jar Binks, cute moppet Darth Vader and all. You can't rub *The Phantom Menace* out of the history of *Star Wars* or the film career of Lucas or the history of film.

Why did Borowczyk accept jobs like helming *The Art of Love* or *Three Immoral Women* or *Emmanuelle 5*, the movies scorned by critics? Partly because filmmakers have to work like anybody else. As the dragon master of Chinese cinema, Tsui Hark, puts it: if you see an opportunity, *take it.*

Come on, it's OK to fail. It's OK to produce rubbish. It's OK to direct porn/ erotica. But to pretend they never happened is just silly.

The film business is *very* cutthroat and *very* competitive: in 1978, for ex, there were about 3,000 filmmakers hoping for a chance to direct one of the 70

25 Yet the Friends of Borowczyk retain *Behind Convent Walls* and *Three Immoral Women,* movies with a high nude/ sex content that's as dubious, it seems, as *The Art of Love* or *Série Rose.*

major movies made in Hollywood that year.

As Julian White put it:

> Walerian Borowczyk had one of the more unusual
> career trajectories in cinema, going from being the
> creator of charming homespun animations to – at
> least in the public mind – a notorious pornographer.
> It's as if Oliver Postgate went from making *The
> Clangers* to directing *Deep Throat*. (2014)

The era of the 1960s and 1970s was a time when
films with graphic sexual content, including porn films,
entered the mainstream, or at least were widely
distributed, and became chic. It was the era of *Deep
Throat, Ai No Corrida, Last Tango In Paris* and *I Am
Curious, Yellow*.[26] It was a time when relaxed censorship
regulations, the new permissiveness, sexual liberation,
increased economic independence for women, audiences
demanding more liberal films, and many other factors,
enabled filmmakers to depict more sex and nudity in
their movies (thus, it was a market-driven movement).
The arty movies were upscale versions of porn –
marketed as 'erotica', not 'porn'; the audience wasn't
solely the raincoat brigade, but dating couples too. It was
a similar audience that might see one of the classier
topless revues in Paris or Las Vegas on a date, after
dinner in a restaurant.

As well as porn manufacturers, 'serious' filmmakers
began to include 'X' rated or 'adult' material. So you
have Bernardo Bertolucci, Alberto Grimaldi and co.
showing sodomy in *Last Tango In Paris*, Anatole
Dauman, Nagima Oshima and co. depicting penetration
in *In the Realm of the Senses*, Pier Paolo Pasolini,
Grimaldi and co. including erections in the 'trilogy of life'
films, and so on. And these were hit movies, too, at the
box office. Film producers like Anatole Dauman (Boro's

---

26 1997's *Boogie Nights* is a marvellous revisit to the Seventies
porn boom.

films) and Alberto Grimaldi[27] (*Last Tango,* Federico Fellini's films, the 'trilogy of life' films of Pasolini), were keenly aware of what audiences wanted to see. Joe Levine had told Jean-Luc Godard in 1963 to put more ass in *Contempt* (as Levine put it), and Godard duly obliged (with scenes of Brigitte Bardot nude). Borowczyk's pictures were very much part of this culture – or at least, they were *received* and *interpreted* within this porn/ art, art film/ porn film context. At times, Borowczyk seems like the reincarnation of the self-appointed Court Pornographer of King Louis XIV.

❁

We have to remind ourselves, in the critical reception of Borowczyk's cinema which emphasizes its erotic or porn aspects, that the films are just as much about a libertarian project, about freedom of expression, about rebelling against the social and political establishment. It's not so much that the movies of Borowczyk and his contemporaries want to depict erotic acts, they want the *freedom* to be able to depict eroticism – and anything else they fancy.

So it's a cinema that takes on the Law of the Father (and the Sins of the Fathers), the older generation, which aims to subvert the political establishment, to transgress social and cultural norms. It's very much part of the æsthetic-political revolution espoused by the Marquis de Sade, by the Surrealists, and taken up in the counterculture and radical movements of the 1960s.

Eroticism, nudity, horror and violence comprises the glossy, sexy, titillating packaging, extreme images developed for marketing, and film producers pandering to the audience. But for the works of Walerian Borowczyk

27 Alberto Grimaldi (1925-2021) produced Pasolini's last four films, from *Il Decamerone* to *Salò*. Grimaldi was a lawyer from Naples; he had formed Produzioni Europee Associate in 1961. He had made plenty of $$$$ by producing the *Fistful of Dollars* Spaghetti Westerns starring Clint Eastwood. Grimaldi went on to become a big cheese in the Italian film industry – producing several Federico Fellini films, for instance, plus *Last Tango In Paris, Novecento, Burn!, Trastevere, Man of La Mancha* and *Storie scellerate.* One of Grimaldi's last producing jobs was *Gangs of New York* (2002). Grimaldi had a distribution deal with United Artists (hence, the films were released thru U.A. in N. America).

et al, that's only one part of the bundle.

❊

Among the regular collaborators in Walerian Borow-czyk's movies were actors such as Marina Pierro and his wife Ligia Branice, DPs Guy Durban and Bernard Daillencourt, production designer Jacques D'Ovidio, Dominique Duvergé (A.D. and production manager), and author André Pieyre de Mandiargues (see below on de Mandiargues).

Walerian Borowczyk's films, like so many European films which have a life outside their country of origin on the international market (only a *tiny* percentage of movies ever get shown outside their country of origin), have a bewildering number of alternative titles. *Docteur Jekyll et les femmes* (1981) was titled *The Blood of Doctor Jeckyll*, *The Bloodbath of Doctor Jeckyll* (the British cut version), *Bloodlust*, *Dr. Jeckyll and His Women* (the North American dubbed version), *Dr. Jeckyll and Miss Osbourne*, and *The Experiment* (the British censored version). Borowczyk's preferred title was *The Strange Case of Dr Jeckyll and Miss Osbourne*. *La Bête* is also known as *The Beast*, *The Beast In Heat* and *Death's Ecstasy*. *Cérémonie d'amour* (1987) was *Queen of the Night* in the U.S.A., and also *Rites of Love* or *Love Rites*. *Les Héroïnes du mal* (1979) is variously *Heroines of Evil*, *Heroines of Pain*, *Immoral Women* and *Three Immoral Women*. *Behind Convent Walls* (*Interno di un convento*, 1978) is also *Sex Life In a Convent* and *Within a Cloister*. *La Marge* (1976) is also *The Margin*, *Emmanuelle '77* and *The Streetwalker*. (Along with the changed titles, producers, studios and distributors also altered scenes, dropped scenes, added scenes, dubbed them, remixed the sound, added music, dropped music, changed the dialogue, etc. Because *they* – *not* the filmmakers – own the movies).

❊

Walerian Borowczyk quickly gained a reputation for producing erotic and (what some people saw as) pornographic material, combined with beautiful, painterly image-making, in which objects and details were given as much weight as people ('I attach a great deal of importance to details', Borowczyk pointed out – but we knew that! [J. Gerber, 173]). I don't regard Borowczyk's films as 'pornographic', 'offensive', etc at all (my own views are resolutely anti-censorship).

There *is* a lot of nudity in the Walerian Borowczyk-directed flicks, compared to the regular Hollywood film, or mainstream flicks in Europe and Asia. But not so extreme when compared to the European art film, which does occasionally have plenty of nudity. Or *mondo/ fantastique/* exploitation cinema.[28] Or porn, of course.

However, it can be historically justified in another respect: go into any major art museum around the world and you'll probably encounter hundreds of naked bodies (Boro has made this very familiar æsthetic point, and of course he was an avid historian of art). From the Renaissance onwards, nudity has been a regular element in high art (and of course in the art of the ancient world). By the time of the 19th century, academy and classical nudes are everywhere. There's Perseus rescuing Andromeda from the serpent, and she's naked; there's Cleopatra/ Aphrodite/ Danaë reclining in her boudoir, and she's naked; there's a bunch of nice, young boys swimming in a river somewhere in France or Spain, and they're naked. And it's obvious that painters and their patrons were choosing mythological or historical or everyday subjects (as opposed to Christian or Biblical ones) precisely so they could depict naked men and women. You couldn't show the Virgin Mary naked, but you could show the Goddess Venus naked. There's no doubt that the fine art nude is in part a classy, upmarket form of lowbrow, populist tits and ass.

If you have a few million dollars to spare and fancied funding some film adaptations of classic erotic books – *Fanny Hill, Moll Flanders, The Romance of Lust, The Perfumed Garden* and of course the *Kama*

28 Junk cinema, trash cinema, *mondo* cinema, has been dubbed 'paracinema' by Jeffrey Sconce, and includes splatterpunk, sword and sandal epics, Elvis Presley films, government hygiene films, beach party musicals, Japanese monster movies, exploitation and *mondo* films.

Sutra – Walerian Borowczyk is without question the filmmaker for the job, in the entire history of cinema.[29]

❀

I've mentioned Walerian Borowczyk in relation to pornography a few times in this book, but the connection lies more in the minds of the people – critics, fans, viewers – watching and discussing Borowczyk's films, than in the films themselves. I don't think the naked human body is pornographic, or showing it is pornographic, and nearly all of so-called pornography is really erotica, designed as entertainment. Rather, the emphasis on extreme violence and suffering in, for instance, contemporary, Hollywood movies, is way more 'pornographic' and disturbing than Borowczyk's films. There's male rape, for example, in movies like *Pulp Fiction, The Shawshank Redemption* and *Deliverance,* and some dubious depictions of sadomasochistic acts in pictures like *Misery, Frenzy,* and *Suspiria.* Even James Bond has been stripped naked and whipped.[30] But those films don't have the stigma of pornography attached to them. And the level of violence and gore in movies such as *Black Hawk Down, Sin City* and *300* is so repulsive, so extreme. There's a sickening emphasis on aggression and physical pain which I regard as psychotic (even in movies rated 'PG-13' and 'PG'. Or 'G'), sometimes dubbed 'torture porn'. It's the kind of thing cultists and martyrs would get off on in the early Christian era – all those religious obsessives who whipped themselves or lived in holes in the ground.

And when you consider action, adventure and blockbuster movies coming out of North America, some of them express a right-wing, pro-military and pro-American ideology and politics which's close to fascism (and white supremacy). And the promoting of North

29 However, the art/ erotic movies backed by porn moguls such as Hugh Heffner and Bob Guccione, have proved disappointing (and, as filmmakers such as Ken Russell found, full of trouble to produce. Russell was involved with an adaptation of *Moll Flanders* by Daniel Defoe, funded by Bob Guccione and the Penthouse company. At the time, Guccione and Penthouse were backing movies (most infamously, *Caligula*). It was a protracted and difficult undertaking, that ended in legal wrangles.)
30 In the completely abysmal *Casino Royale* (2006).

American political and ideological aggression is deeply disturbing – some movies are virtually adverts for the military machine.[31] ('America Über Alles', I call it).

❀

Information on Walerian Borowczyk is scant, to say the least. I mean, way flimsier than many other lesser-known filmmakers. You have to really hunt and dig around, while his contemporaries, such as Pier Paolo Pasolini or Jean-Luc Godard, have whole cultural industries devoted to them.

As for books on Walerian Borowczyk – there aren't any. Why? We all have our theories, but Borowczyk's cinema simply hasn't compelled the film community, the critical academy, the universities, wherever, to devote much time or effort to it.

OK, there have been 1 or 2 books about Borowczyk,[32] but for such a major talent, it's too few. Where's the study of Borowczyk's cinema in terms of psychoanalysis, Freud and Lacan? (That would write itself!) Where's the detailed study of his animation and short films? Where's the deconstruction of the themes of power and politics in Borowczyk's work? (However, don't hold your breath for a sympathetic feminist critique of Borowczyk's output!).

Of sources that are readily available, I'd recommend David Cook's *A History of Narrative Film* – for me it's the finest single book on cinema around. There's a useful chapter on Walerian Borowczyk in *Immoral Tales: Sex and Horror Cinema in Europe 1956-1984*, by Cathal Tohill and Pete Tombs, a really marvellous movie book. About the best introduction to Boro you'll find. Jacques Gerber's book on the film producer Anatole Dauman includes a section on Borowczyk. Michael Richardson has a chapter on Boro in his *Surrealism and Cinema* (details on these books are in the bibliography).

Walerian Borowczyk is often mentioned in guide-books to European and world cinema, but the entries are usually short and not particularly enlightening, merely repeating the same facts (fab Polish animator who turned

31 Sometimes dubbed 'combat porn'.
32 But some're out of print.

to features, helmed some intriguing early works (*Goto, Blanche*), before being sidetracked into Euro-ero-trash). Similarly, on the internet, there is information on Borowczyk, but not much, and so websites that I would recommend are few. Internet Movie Database (imdb.com) is always good, and Senses of Cinema, and the Movie Review Query Engine (mrqe.com).[33] I have included a filmography of Borowczyk, because apart from places like the Internet Movie Database, it's difficult to find.

In short, Walerian Borowczyk deserves to be much better known in film circles, and his movies deserve to be seen. But his films seem destined to be lumped with exploitation cinema, softcore porn, *mondo* cinema, *fantastique* cinema, and arthouse cinema, perpetually on the outer reaches of world cinema. (And Borowczyk's films are difficult to track down; only a proportion are currently available in Europe and the U.S.A., and you'll need to search hard to find them).

Yet Boro is not alone: several major filmmakers have been very poorly served by full-length studies: F.W. Murnau, Hayao Miyazaki, and Katsuhiro Otomo.

---

33 There's a terrific gallery of Borowczyk's art at Animation World Network: awm.com/ gallery/boro/info

Walerian Borowczyk

DEUX HEURES avec WALERIAN BOROWCZ

Dans le cadre de l'exposition CAMERA OBSCURA
présentation des ____ d'animation :

était une fois, Les _____gutes, _____
Les Jeux _____es, e'_____

____AINE à 21 h.   S____anche PERM____

The talented Ligia Branice in two images
by her husband Walerian Borowczyk; a portrait
and from Goto: Island of Love.

André Pieyre de Mandiargues (in 1958)

CONTES IMMORAUX

scénario et réalisation
WALERIAN BOROWCZYK

Visa ministériel n° 41659

The rather plain, even austere title card for Immoral Tales.
White on black, it might be an Ingmar Bergman or Woody Allen movie.

UNMADE BOROWCZYK PROJECTS

Like many filmmakers, Walerian Borowczyk had projects he wanted to produce, but didn't, or couldn't (Borowczyk had his share of struggling to raise finance, and battling with film producers. It's a familiar story you hear with almost every important filmmaker). The unmade Boro projects included:

▲ A film about Frédéric Chopin and Géorges Sand (the subject of several film/ TV works), budgeted at $7 million. It would've combined several Borowczykian themes – music, obsession, Europe and the 19th century.

▲ *Nefertiti* – developed in the 1980s, with Borowczyk's actress muse Marina Pierro to star.[1] It would've been set in Ancient Egypt. (Boro dived into Ancient Rome instead, in *Ars Amandi*). A Nefertiti film was made in Italy – *Nefertite, Queen of the Nile* (1961).

▲ Gilles de Rais, the notorious serial killer (with Udo Keir to star – this was when Boro first met Keir. Instead, he moved on to *Lulu* and then *The Strange Case of Dr. Jeckyll and Miss Osbourne*).

No doubt Boro turned down many film offers over the course of his career (but he did answer calls occasionally – most notoriously in the case of film producer Alain Siritsky and *Emmanuelle 5*). One wishes that Borowczyk hadn't had to struggle so much to get projects off the ground (particularly in the 1980s) – but many filmmakers suffered the same fate, even giants like Orson Welles, Carl-Theodor Dreyer and Mickey Powell. (How could you *not* give Dreyer money to film his cherished *Jesus* project? Or to Welles to film his long-planned *King Lear*? Couldn't we trade a single $150 million U.S. blockbuster movie (seen once, instantly forgotten), for the unmade films of Dreyer, Welles, Ken Russell, Andrei Tarkovsky, and Borowczyk? Just one of those ultra-high budget productions would pay for many unmade films of so many directors!).

It could've been marvellous, too, if Walerian Borowczyk had taken on some genres and forms of

1 A Nefertiti production appeared in 1995.

cinema far from his comfort zone: a Borowczyk Western! A Borowczyk space opera! And my own choice for Boro: a full-on, stops-all-out musical, complete with elaborate dance numbers and wild choreography (indeed, the film musical form, with its emphasis on set design, on costumes, on props, on lighting, on visual effects and cinematic trickery, and the whole look – plus of course music – is perfect for Borowczyk. Or a particular form of musical movie – the Bollywood musical or *masala* movie, a killer combo of slapstick comedy, over-the-top action, visual effects, intense romance, hysterical melodrama, plus songs and dances).

The other genre or format which would be fascinating to see Boro have a stab at is a comedy: the closest we have is *The Beast*, I suppose, or parts of *Mr and Mrs Kabal*. Boro had a wicked sense of humour (leaning towards black humour, sometimes very dark), but to apply that to a feature-length movie, couched entirely as a comedy, might've been wild.

All of Walerian Borowczyk's live-action productions were made with low to medium budgets (in the European system; in the U.S. system, *very* low budgets): one wonders what Boro might've done with a truly colossal canvas – with a cast of thousands, with multiple locations, with a visual effects budget of $80 million. If Boro had been given a film of the scale of *The Leopard* (1963) or *The Bible* (1966), for instance.

A final dream: putting Walerian Borowczyk in charge of a team of 400 animators and a large budget. After all, there have been some maverick animators who've worked in the upper end of the budgetary scale – Henry Selick (*Nightmare Before Christmas, James and the Giant Peach, Monkeybone*) and Ralph Bakshi (*Fritz the Cat, Lord of the Rings, Wizards*). Certainly Tim Burton and Selick have produced stop-motion animations (together and separately) with Borowczykian ingredients (*Frankenweenie, Corpse Bride, Nightmare Before Christmas*), and Bakshi has cleverly capitalized on his outsider, counter-culture status in the film business. Meanwhile, animators such as Jan Svankmajer have managed to survive and make animated works by developing suitable financial deals and practical resources.

TWO BOROWCZYKS

There are two Walerian Borowczyks exalted by fans and critics: there are those who venerate Borowczyk the animator, the Borowczyk who produced the early animated shorts, the Borowczyk who can be placed alongside animators such as Jiri Trnka and Jan Svankmajer, the Borowczyk who's linked to the Surrealists, the *avant garde*, Georges Bataille, blah blah blah. For these devotees of Boro (many are based in Paris), the works enshrined are:
- The short films
- *Mr. and Mrs. Kabal's Theatre*
- *Goto: Island of Love*
- *Blanche*

Blanche is the cut-off point – 1972 – before Walerian Borowczyk's cinema is tainted/ sidetracked by erotica/ sexual issues, or when erotica unbalances the mix, and critics find it harder to justify their exaltation of Boro (within two years, Borowczyk shifted from prestige, Bressonian historical drama to out-there erotica, from *Blanche* to *Immoral Tales*). At a pinch, *Immoral Tales, The Streetwalker, Lulu* and *The Story of Sin* might be included in the critical *œuvre* (meanwhile, *The Beast* can't be ignored, but it's a long way from the *avant garde*/ animator/ Surrealist Borowczyk).

Many great filmmakers have produced only short films (or mainly short films), however: Stan Brakhage, Maya Deren, Jordan Belson, and Kenneth Anger. And in the silent cinema era, most films were short – one reel, two reels, three reels (certainly in the first half of the silent era).

A film can be a masterpiece if it's only a minute long (*Mothlight* by Stan Brakhage, for instance), or 2m 20s (*Stellar,* also by Brakhage). *Scorpio Rising* and *Lucifer Rising,* the films-as-magickal-rituals of Kenneth Anger, are super-intense, but not feature-length – and they don't need to be, either.

Back to the Other Boro: then there's the Walerian Borowczyk who directed crazy, erotic movies like *Immoral Tales, Three Immoral Women, Behind Convent Walls, The Art of Love* and *The Beast.* For the fans and critics who enjoy these works, Borowczyk is just another of the many European directors who delivered arty porn, or sexy art flicks – like Pier Paolo Pasolini, Bernardo Bertolucci and Ken Russell (at the top end), and Jess Franco, Tinto Brass and Jean Rollin (lower down the critical scale). For these aficionados, the movies of note are:

- *Immoral Tales*
- *The Beast*
- *The Streetwalker*
- *Behind Convent Walls*
- *Three Immoral Women*
- *Dr Jeckyll*
- *The Art of Love*
- *Emmanuelle 5*
- *Love Rites*

The fans and critics (the intellectuals and nerds) who enshrine the early, Surrealist, *avant garde* Borowczyk ('Borowczyk the Artist'), wish to God (or to Jupiter, Isis, Jehovah, Allah, Athena, etc), that he hadn't put his name to *Three Immoral Women, The Art of Love* and, worst of all, *Emmanuelle 5.* (These are the folk who pretend that *Emmanuelle 5* never happened, and try to erase it from the Myth and Legend of W. Borowczyk. Maybe if Boro had moved from *Immoral Tales* to *The Story of Sin,* missing out *The Beast,* and later films such as *Behind Convent Walls* and *Three Immoral Women,* and headed from *The Story of Sin* to *Dr Jeckyll,* his reputation wouldn't have been damaged seemingly beyond repair. *Immoral Tales* might be seen as an aberration, then, with

Boro getting back to 'serious' cinema with *The Story of Sin*).

The fans and critics who enjoy the nudie, porny Borowczyk flicks, couldn't give a ¡¢%# about 'Art' and the European, intellectual *avant garde* (with its élitist, snooty, self-important attitude towards 'low brow' or crude culture). It can be pointed out, and easily proved, that Walerian Borowczyk as a director included nudity and sex in every single one of his live-action features from *Immoral Tales* onwards (not discussions of (or references to) nudity and sexuality in dialogue, but nude bodies and sex acts portrayed on screen). Every one of them (and there's gratuitous nudity in *Goto* (the scene of the hookers bathing nude is completely unnecessary), and women are objectified in *The Theatre of Mr and Mrs Kabal*). And the main characters are nude or in sex scenes in most of Borowczyk's movies. And some projects were definitely conceived by the producers – Braunberger, Dauman, Siritsky, etc[2] (not the director) to feature sex and nudity as a key element: *The Beast, Immoral Tales, Behind Convent Walls, La Marge, Emmanuelle 5, Three Immoral Women, The Art of Love, Love Rites* and *Softly From Paris*. Which's over half of Boro's feature/drama output.

There's an unease among film critics about Walerian Borowczyk: should they celebrate a film director who concentrates so much on eroticism? Yes, but it's quite OK for film criticism to worship filmmakers who fetishize violence (Sam Peckinpah, John Woo, Ringo Lam, William Friedkin, Michael Mann), or crime (Alfred Hitchcock, Beat Kitano), or gangsters (Martin Scorsese, Abel Ferrara), or horror (John Carpenter, George Romero, Dario Argento, Wes Craven), or childish nonsense (Walt Disney, Steven Spielberg, George Lucas, James Cameron).

In short, some film genres and forms are not regarded as highly as others: comedy, horror, porn, erotica and exploitation are near the bottom of the critical-cultural hierarchy, with drama, history and

2 So you could also argue that film producers like Anatole Dauman and Alain Siritsky led Borowczyk astray, pushing him towards featuring too many erotic elements.

tragedy at the top. Makers of comedy films bemoan their under-valued status, yet you can argue that a humorous view of life is even more important for health and well-being than 'serious' drama or tragedy, with its Aristotlean, psychological catharsis.

But it's not just the inclusion of erotic or porno-graphic material in Boro's cinema that leads critics to demean it, it's *how* he used erotica: it's unexpected, or too intense, or too unusual, and it departs from the cultural norms (if it were sited within, say, a romantic drama, it might be 'justified', narratively).

Some important filmmakers of Walerian Boro-wczyk's generation have produced several films featuring a *lot* of explicit material, yet their reputations have remained very high. Pier Paolo Pasolini is the obvious comparison: his 'trilogy of life' films of the 1970s, for instance. Yet these movies – *The Decameron* (*Il Decamerone*, 1971), *The Canterbury Tales* (*I Racconti di Canterbury*, 1972) and *The Arabian Nights* (*Il Fiore Delle Mille a Una Notte*, 1974) – contain some truly awful filmmaking. Parts of *The Canterbury Tales* are so bad (the direction is often inept, the acting ranges from mediocre to terrible, and the script is really poor), you can't believe they were produced by the white-hot director of *The Gospel According To Matthew* or *Accattone*. Yet Pasolini is revered as a God among filmmakers, and he continues to receive an enormous amount of critical attention. (And yet Pasolini's film career is very patchy in places: *Pigsty, Love Meetings* and *The Hawks and the Sparrows*. If you include parts of the 'trilogy of life' films, that's a high proportion out of Pasolini's thirteen features – the same number of films as Borowczyk. Also, Pasolini was involved in several scandals and court cases as a youth and a school teacher, including accusations of sex with minors. Yet that hasn't dented his superstar status).

And Bernardo Bertolucci, from a subsequent gener-ation (18 years younger than Borowczyk), foregrounded sexual material many times (*Last Tango In Paris, 1900, La Luna, The Sheltering Sky, The Dreamers*, etc). Yet

Bertolucci's critical status remains high (even tho' sections of his films are as dodgy and as exploitative as Borowczyk's films).

DEFENDING BOROWCZYK

The legend of Walerian Borowczyk's feature film career has the Polish film director starting strongly in live-action – *Goto* and *Blanche* – but declining by the late 1970s into arty erotica (*Three Immoral Women, Behind Convent Walls*), reviving a tad (*Dr Jeckyll, Lulu*), only to skid again (*The Art of Love*), crashing headlong into the colossal pile of steaming dreck that is *Emmanuelle 5*.

But I'm going to defend Borowczyk here: plenty of 'major' film directors have produced turkeys – movies that're cack-handed, badly-conceived and sometimes offensively pro-militaristic. Such as, among recent movies (1980s-present):

Steven Spielberg, *Tin-Tin* (some would add *Hook* and *1941*)

Ridley Scott, *Hannibal* (cost: $87 million),[3] *Kingdom of Heaven, G.I. Jane*

Sam Raimi, *Spider-man 3*

Peter Greenaway, *8 1/2 Women*

Peter Jackson, *The Hobbit, King Kong, The*

---

3 *Hannibal* (2001), part of the *Silence of the Lambs*/ Thomas Harris franchise, was overseen by film legend Dino de Laurentiis (1919-2010). *Hannibal* was a pitifully bad thriller, woefully misjudged in tone and substance. It's difficult to believe that Ridley Scott directed it, and that David Mamet and Steve Zallian worked on the screenplay (*Steve Zallian*! He wrote *Schindler's List*! Much-celebrated playwright *David Mamet*!). Some critics agree with me: 'very likely the worst film of this year and quite possibly the next', commented Charles Taylor in Salon.com, while Ella Taylor in *L.A. Weekly* called it 'the flabbiest of cop-outs'. Mick LaSalle in the *San Francisco Chronicle* found *Hannibal* 'wilfully gross, fundamentally stupid and in no way worth the discomfit of watching it.'
According to Wikipedia, the budget for *Hannibal* was $87 million. 87,000,000 bucks! You have GOT to be kidding! For a routine thriller that would cost less than a million on TV!

Frighteners

Brian de Palma, *The Bonfire of the Vanities, Snake Eyes, Mission To Mars*

Paul Thomas Anderson, *Punch-Drunk Love, There Will Be Blood*

Joel Schumacher, *8MM*

Alan Parker, *Evita*

Terry Gilliam, *The Brothers Grimm, Fear and Loathing In Las Vegas*

Quentin Tarantino, *Kill Bill*

(Most of those film directors are clearly not 'major', and not in Borowczyk's class).

And how about these turkeys? (there are *thousands* more) –

The Lion, the Witch and The Wardrobe (cost: $180m)

Prince Caspian (cost: $200m)

Voyage of the Dawn Treader (cost: $140-155m)

Home On the Range (cost: $110m)

Snow White and the Huntsman (cost: $170 million!)[4]

Raise the Titanic (cost: $40m)[5]

Quantum of Solace

Casino Royale (2006)[6]

The Avengers (1997)[7]

Batman Begins

King Arthur

---

4 A complete flop, *Snow White and the Huntsman* (Universal, 2012), is... a series of empty shots, a fairy tale eviscerated of all magic. There's literally *nothing here*, nothing going on. I wait and wait for *something* to happen. But it doesn't.

What a waste of money! *Snow White* isn't 'bloated' or over-done or OTT (some of the usual accusations against current blockbuster flicks), it's not 'done' at all (it's uncooked). It's just empty. There really is nothing there at all.

5 Come on, the model of the *Titanic* ship alone cost seven million bucks!

6 The *James Bond* re-boot which had the sophisticated, world-weary super-spy acting like a ditzy, love-sick teenager.

7 *The Avengers* (1997) was a stunningly inept, miserable, mis-cast and misconceived train wreck.

Where the Wild Things Are[8]

The Beach

The Hunger Games[9]

Amélie

Alien vs. Predator[10]

the *Bourne* series

Chocolat[11]

Vanilla Sky

About a Boy

Billy Elliot

The Hulk (2003)[12]

Legend (1985)[13]

Howard the Duck (cost: $34m)

Fantastic Beasts

Lolita (cost: $62m!)

Lara Croft ($90m)

Charlie's Angels (cost: $90m)

Oceans 11

Unbreakable

Jungle Book 2

Lemony Snicket

The Cat In the Hat

Sin City

The Village

X-Men Origins: Wolverine[14]

Bridget Jones

---

8 Universal's cretinous movie-as-psychotherapy, offensive on every possible level.

9 *The Hunger Games* was a piece of adolescent claptrap cobbled together from *Lord of the Flies, The Truman Show, Westworld, Battle Royale*, reality TV and Ancient Rome. *The Hunger Games* comes over as a third-rate TV movie but far less fun (too frigging long and no ad breaks!). A limp, bloodless satire on North America's slack-jawed consumption of reality television (and the media in general), groups of people lost on islands, and a bunch of silly games in which death is the only way out.

10 A shockingly naff destruction of a once-prestigious franchise.

11 Despite a stellar cast that includes Juliet Binoche and Johnny Depp, *Chocolat* is almost unendurable.

12 Simply awful and woefully misjudged (despite the high-calibre talent involved).

13 *Legend* (1985) was an abysmal attempt at a fairy tale movie that cost $30 million to make, but took only $15.5m domestically.

14 A deeply disturbing cesspit of a movie.

Speed 2 (cost: $110m)[15]
The Da Vinci Code[16]

Some of the pictures noted above are not only shockingly bad, they are also mind-bogglingly expensive ($270-350 million for *Spiderman 3*?! Or *The Hobbit*?!!), but can anybody remember anything about *Voyage of the Dawn Treader, Lara Croft, Home On the Range, Bridget Jones, King Arthur* or *The Village* now? (They provided some great material for spoofs, though).

Apart from the irredeemable *Emmanuelle 5*, even Walerian Borowczyk's lowest ebbs were not as dreadful as *Speed 2, Where the Wild Things Are, Bridget Jones, The Da Vinci Code, Quantum of Solace, Kill Bill, Hannibal, The Avengers, Billy Elliot, Legend, The Hunger Games,* the *Narnia* pictures, *Chocolat, Snow White* or *Lolita* (Boro could've made this last picture about a middle-aged man and his under-age obsession for $500,000, not $62 million! – and it would've been 1,000 times more enjoyable!).

Add up the negative costs, the above-the-line costs, and the P. & A. costs of just one or two of those turkeys, and you'd have enough dough to pay for *all* of Borowczyk's unmade, long-cherished film projects! Instead of *Chocolat, The Hunger Games* and *Where the Wild Things Are* (like, who gives a hoot about those movies?!), we'd have (among others):

Nefertiti – a $18 million Ancient Egyptian epic starring Marina Pierro.

Chopin and Sand – a lavish ($7m) doomed romance about Frédéric Chopin and Géorges Sand.

(And we could say to Boro, no, don't direct *Emmanuelle 5*, we can offer you something much better: here's the $18 million you wanted to make *Nefertiti*).

---

15 *Speed 2* (1997, Fox) defies belief for its inadequacy in all areas of filmmaking and conception. How it grossed $48,068,396 in the U.S.A. is anybody's guess.
16 While we're talking about movie duds, how about *The Da Vinci Code*? 'A humourless drudge of a movie, endured by most audiences rather than enjoyed', as Mark Kermode put it (*Hatchet Job*, Picador, 2013, 278).

WALERIAN BOROWCZYK, WOMEN AND PORNOGRAPHY

Walerian Borowczyk was a *connoisseur* of erotica, as his films bear out, and had a small collection of erotic objects. Like many an erotic art addict, Borowczyk was in love with the female form and sex. His movies are full of images of naked or semi-nude women, like painterly studies out of the *œuvres* of Jean Auguste Dominique Ingres, Titian or Peter Paul Rubens, the camera often lingering on their pudenda and pubic hair, their breasts, or close-ups of their mouths. Often, Borowczyk's film-women are alone, engaging in autoerotic, narcissistic acts, like the women in high art: bathing, admiring themselves in a mirror, or, unlike in high art, caressing some object, and masturbating. Few filmmakers have featured as many images of masturbation, particularly female masturbation, in their works as Walerian Borowczyk (occurring in seven of Borowczyk's 13 features, plus in the *Série Rose* TV series).

Walerian Borowczyk favoured slim, young women in his films. At least in the lead roles. The fleshly, curvy figures of the art of Aristide Maillol or Eric Gill or the 19th century academy nude are much rarer in his cinema. He didn't go for the large forms of Russ Meyer, either (and Borowczyk's camera lingers more over hips, asses and vulvas than breasts. His cinema fetishizes mouths, memorably – a recurring motif in all of Boro's cinema). Borowczyk favoured white women, rather than black or Asian women.

For Sigmund Freud, the fetish was a substitute for the missing penis of the mother, a view that perpetuated the fantasy of the phallic mother. In her essay "Fetishization", Elizabeth Grosz is illuminatingly clear:

> The fetishist demands, in spite of recognizing its impossibility, that there be a maternal phallus. He simultaneously affirms and denies that the mother is castrated... Fetishization renders the object into an image of another, genital object, thereby sexual-izing it and making it into an appropriate or worthy

object of desire for the subject. It thus describes a common male mode of objectification of women's bodies. (1992, 117)

Walerian Borowczyk has never been simply a high-class eroticist, as his detractors have asserted (I don't regard him as a pornographer at all – but a lover of erotica, certainly). He shoots from a finished script, and pays special attention to the set, the design, and the many unusual props and objects in the frame. (It would take a long time to find and rent/ buy all the props and furniture for a Borowczyk movie; indeed, some of the props were constructed by the maestro himself. Very few professional directors build their own props!).

But the critical perception of Walerian Borowczyk's cinema seems to have been over-shadowed by the nudity and erotic elements, with viewers and critics seeing that and not much else. A pity, because there's so much more going on in Borowczyk's films than nude bodies and fucking. And there's also a feeling among detractors that Borowczyk wasted his talent on worthless films. So that his career begins strongly, with *Goto: Island of Love*, *Blanche* and *Immoral Tales,* but deteriorates to the crass level of *Emmanuelle 5*. There's a view among film critics that Borowczyk would have done so much better if he'd concentrated on some really challenging subjects, something that was worthy of his talent; if he had continued with a respectable film career like, say. Chris Marker or Alain Resnais.

(Why do so many critics and fans talk about the eroticism and nudity in the cinema of Walerian Borowczyk and not the thousands of other elements? Because it's *fun*. See, for many people, movies are *entertainment*. They are *stories*. They don't go to movies for philosophical treatises, for 'messages', for political diatribes, for radical deconstructions of society, etc.)

That's one view. Fine. OK.

But the facts don't bear it out. For instance, *Love Rites*, released in 1987, is a great Walerian Borowczyk film – the equal, I'd say, with *The Story of Sin* (1975). So it wasn't really a 'decline' into mediocrity and dirty, old man territory, because *Love Rites* shows Borowczyk enjoying himself immensely with a tale of guy who gets involved with a prostitute in modern-day Paris and discovers more than he bargained for. *Love Rites* is not porn, not smut, not a sleazy, old man leching after acres of young, naked flesh.

And since the late 1990s and early 2000s, there has been a liberalization in film censorship/ classification (in Europe), and the 'N.C.-17' rating (in the U.S.A.), with a bunch of films reaching more mainstream markets which have been trumpeted for containing more sexually explicit material. Yes, you can see genitals at play in films like *Romance, Intimacy, Pola X, Love, 9 Songs* and others, but those movies aren't a patch on even the lesser Borowczyk films.[17] (The liberalization is of course linked to late capitalism, to the marketplace, as the movie industry moves through more cycles).

Also, let's remember that the turn towards erotica – from *Blanche* to *Immoral Tales*, was not instigated by Walerian Borowczyk, but by film producer Anatole Dauman and Argos Films. It was Dauman and Argos who asked Borowczyk to come up with some stories to make an anthology of erotic material, which led to *Immoral Tales*. (And when Borowczyk had fulfilled the contract of two films for Dauman – *Immoral Tales* and *The Beast* – Borowczyk went back to a form closer to straight drama, with *The Story of Sin*. However, that movie, it's true, contains numerous nude and partially nude scenes, not all of which are justified by the material and themes).

Is Walerian Borowczyk's cinema sexist or misogynist? It's hardly worth even bothering to address the question, because most every feminist or critic who looks at Borowczyk's films will be certain of their out-and-out chauvinism and apparent misogynism. A feminist would say: 'is there a moment in Borowczyk's cinema when it *isn't* misogynist or sexist?'

For example, it's striking just how many incidents there are of women being put in cages, or locked up in

17 Except for the dreaded *Emmanuelle 5*!

Boro's cinema: *Blanche, Série Rose, Goto, Behind Convent Walls, Three Immoral Women, Immoral Tales,* etc. And prostitutes appear in most of Walerian Borowczyk's feature movies, from *Goto* to *Love Rites* (including *Immoral Tales, The Story of Sin, The Streetwalker, Three Immoral Women, Lulu* and *The Art of Love*). And there are several rapes.[18] Dear reader, these are not scenes that endear themselves to feminists!

Walerian Borowczyk's films as director and co-writer contain plenty of ammunition for evidence of fear, anxiety, neurosis and all the rest of it about women. But misogynism is not part of Borowczyk's cinema or philosophy. The opposite, in fact (but feminists counter that worshipping women can be as inappropriate/ ignorant/ negative as disliking and fearing them).

What's striking, though, while we're on the subject of women, gender and feminism, is just how many of Walerian Borowczyk's films feature women in the lead roles (and sometimes they are strong women, or women with a significant agency or independence): *Blanche, Three Immoral Women, Immoral Tales, The Beast, The Story of Sin, The Streetwalker, Emmanuelle 5, Lulu, Behind Convent Walls, The Art of Love, Love Rites* – actually, it's *all* of Borowczyk's live-action films, apart from *Goto: Island of Love* and *Dr Jeckyll*. And that makes Borowczyk *very* unusual for a male film director, and for any major filmmaker.

For all its apparent sexism and misogynism, Walerian Borowczyk's cinema contains some strong roles for women. Miriam Gwen in *Love Rites*, for instance, may be a sadistic prostitute, but she's also a strong, independent woman. And at the end of *La Bête* it's the two Beasts that die, while the heroines survive (though damaged).

▲

Femme fatales are one of Walerian Borowczyk's specialities in film – Miriam Gwen in *Love Rites* is the last in a series of many *femme fatales*, women who

18 Sometimes in the same film – *Three Immoral Women*, for example.

aren't just naughty (Lucrezia Borgia), they kill (Marceline, Margherita, Fanny Osbourne), and some slaughter *en masse* (Erzsébet Báthory).

Both Borowczyk and his co-conspirator in the realm of the erotic and the Surreal, André Pieyre de Mandiargues, would be very familiar with the *femme fatale* type (and Paris, their home town, is world central for the *femme fatale* in art).

The *femme fatale* type neatly melds issues such as sex and death,[19] desire and fear, contact and loss, for the (male) artist. And sex and pain, sadism and masochism. She is the Freudian, castrating mother, the toothed vagina, the decapitating Goddess Kali.

Consider, in Walerian Borowczyk's cinema, Fanny Osbourne at the end of *The Strange Case of Dr. Jeckyll and Miss Osbourne*, stabbing her mother in a frenzy and licking the knife; 'La Fornarina' dispatching Raphael Sanzio and Bernardo Bini in *Three Immoral Women*; Marceline slashing her parents (in the same flick); Miriam Gwen clawing at Hugo as she rides him orgasmically in *Love Rites*; and Countess Báthory bathing in the blood of twenty-five virgins in *Immoral Tales*.

The *femme fatale* appears in mythology and art in figures such as Medusa, Salomé, Delilah, Jezebel, Judith, Lilith, Ninuë (the lover of Merlin), Venus, Lucrezia, Helen of Troy, La Belle Dame Sans Merci and Cleopatra (Boro's cinema alludes to several of those *femme fatales*). These female types combined beauty with death, immense power and all manner of sadistic, masochistic and fetishistic fantasies. These are the women who will whip you to death, if you wish, as in Leopold von Sacher-Masoch's *Venus In Furs* (Borowczyk's last feature-length

19 Women and death are merged throughout Western art, including in the works of Walerian Borowczyk. In many Symbolist pictures, for instance, the figure of death with the sickle is a woman, as in Odilon Redon's *Death: My Irony Surpasses All Others*, 1889 (from Gustave Flaubert's *The Temptation of St. Anthony*; another key work of the Symbolist/ Decadent era); Félicien Rops: *Mors Syphilitica*, Bibliothéque Nationale, Paris; Alfred Kubin: *The Best Medicine*, 1901-2, private collection; and Paul Gauguin: *Madame La Mort*, 1899, Musée d'Orsay.

film, *Love Rites,* is in part a version of *Venus In Furs*).

The *femme fatale* is one of the main female types in 19th century art: there are many variations on the same basic type; the woman as death, as a prostitute, as a dominatrix, a temptress, a queen, a warrior, an Amazon, the serpent, the mermaid, the vampire, the sphinx, etc. *Femme fatales* appear in the art of Arnold Böcklin, Dante Gabriel Rossetti, Franz von Stück, Félicien Rops and perhaps the greatest artist of the type – Gustave Moreau.

▲

I wouldn't say that the chauvinism/ sexism was any worse in Walerian Borowczyk's films than, say, the films of Jean-Luc Godard or Rainer Maria Fassbinder or Federico Fellini or many European art filmmakers (have a look at *Contempt* or *Prénom: Carmen* dir. by Godard, for instance, or *City of Women* or *8 1/2* dir. by Fellini). But the chauvinism certainly is more overt, more obvious in Borowczyk's cinema; it reveals the sexism, the patriarchal laws, the social hierarchies in which women are secondary participants, much more vividly than many other European movies of the same era.

Having considered Walerian Borowczyk's films for some time, I wonder if one of the reasons that some viewers find the concentration on sex and nudity off-putting is the way that Borowczyk and the production teams incorporate it. Sex scenes and nudity are regular elements in movies – at least in the Western tradition, and have been since cinema was invented (early pioneers such as D.W. Griffith and Cecil B. DeMille included nude scenes). But in Borowczyk's films, the camera lingers over parts of the body far, far longer than most movies do. And the films employ not one shot of a butt or a mound, but many. Hold on anything like that for too long and some viewers get uncomfortable. It's not that they can't look at nude bodies, whether male, female or whatever, it's that Borowczyk's films put viewers into a particular viewing position which makes their voyeurism, their collusion, palpable. (Or is that today people are more squeamish about the body? In mediaeval times, where religion predominated, swearing and bad language revolved around God or the gods, not parts of the body, as today [20]).

❀

Walerian Borowczyk cast beautiful women in his leading roles: Sylvia Kristel, Ligia Branice, and Marina Pierro. If you were cast in a Borowczyk film, you'd be expected to strip off – completely (no body suits, no special clothes to hide bits you don't want to show). You'd probably have to do a sex scene, and also some homosexual/ lesbian sex. You might have to run through fields or woods naked (and barefoot). But Boro and his casting assistants certainly had a knack for discovering terrific unknown actors (and performers willing to do a lot of crazy stuff).[21]

There's more humour than one might think in Walerian Borowczyk's films. Not understanding the humour is part of the problem with viewing films with subtitles or dubbing (to test this – watch a movie in a language you don't understand with an audience that does understand it. You'll see a difference between the subtitles you don't think are particularly funny and the audience laughing). Humour is a tough ingredient to translate – which's why someone like Stephen Chow (Chow Sing-chi) can be a mega-star in Asia but virtually unknown in the West.

But true eroticism, Walerian Borowczyk said, doesn't like laughter or jokes. True eroticism was a serious business, he remarked. Borowczyk though couldn't resist adding humour to sexual situations. He called *The Beast* more a comedy than an erotic film.

The humour in Borowczyk's films, tho', is not gags or scripted routines, but a wry, ironic (and sometimes bleak) look at life. It's very intelligent, very educated humour.

A film director who has employed even more nudity than Walerian Borowczyk – in terms of sheer numbers –

20 See Dan Jones, *Realm Divided*, Head of Zeus, 2015, 64.
21 Some of them only appeared in Boro's films and nothing else – Pier Paolo Pasolini has the same nose for discovering amazing unprofessional actors – and often the actors only worked in Pasolini's films and nowhere else.

is Peter Greenaway. There are similarities between Borowczyk and Greenaway, but not in the use of nudity and sex. In Greenaway's cinema naked bodies are presented in a cool, even cold, scientific and medical fashion. They are arranged as out of historical paintings but they look like people queuing up to be medically examined. Borowczyk's approach is much more openly erotic (or more erotically open – less judgemental). He loves naked bodies (and not only women's bodies). In Greenaway's cinema there's a feeling of the filmmaker being ashamed or restrained even as he's fascinated by nudity. He wants to be a *European* filmmaker but can't quite shake off his repressed, *British* side. In Borowczyk's cinema, he doesn't care about repression and such things, and is happy to linger at length over nude bodies.

MAKING A BOROWCZYK FILM

What was it like making a Walerian Borowczyk film? Here are some guesses, partly based on accounts from the casts and crews. I don't know for sure, but I bet the hours were long on a Borowczyk shoot; I bet Borowczyk would carry on filming until he got what he wanted. I bet the actors had to rough it along with the crew (no cosy trailers, no comfy limos ferrying actors from plush hotels miles away). I bet Borowczyk wouldn't have any time for actors who didn't want to do what they'd already agreed to do (like stripping off or having sex or jumping out of a boat). I bet actors were expected to throw themselves into the roles with no holding back. I bet there were no hour-long, Method acting discussions about 'motivation' or 'back-story' on set.[22]

It's likely that filming with Walerian Borowczyk was the first time that many actors (certainly among the non-

22 But if Boro fancied holding up shooting while he himself re-painted a piece of the set, that was fine.

professionals) had encountered a film director like this. Veterans like Pierre Brasseur and Michel Simon had no doubt been on a few film sets with some oddballs.

I bet Walerian Borowczyk was meticulous to the point of driving everyone else in the crew nuts (I can imagine Borowczyk art directing scenes to the point of maddening detail – adjusting the way the folds in a dress lay on a bed, for instance, or having a painting hang on a wall *just so*). The actress Grazyna Dlugolecka (*The Story of Sin*) commented that Borowczyk moved actors around like pawns, and seemed to be more concerned with how props looked.[23] Other observers have noted that Boro seemed to view actors as puppets or as figures in one of his animations. I bet Borowczyk inspired a kind of grudging respect in his cast and crew (and there would be no doubt over who was top dog on set).

It seems that Walerian Borowczyk shot everything, too, and didn't hand over filming to second unit directors or assistants.[24] In other words, you can sense Borowczyk's presence behind every scene. Sex film producer Alain Siritsky said that Borowczyk 'can do everything: write, lighting, set design, edit and even do the poster'.[25] (Boro seems to be one of those filmmakers who can also do everyone else's job better than they can – except, of course, acting, the one area of cinema where even the very greatest film directors have to acknowledge their limitations). Only one diva was allowed on set – and that was Borowczyk (the same is true of Ken Russell, Pier Paolo Pasolini, Cecil B. DeMille and D.W. Griffith).

I imagine that producers and crew, as with Orson Welles or Alfred Hitchcock, wouldn't interfere with Walerian Borowczyk's vision once the film had been agreed upon and was shooting (Borowczyk did not like to be contradicted during shooting – what director does?!). Borowczyk knew what he was doing and I bet producers[26] and crew found it easier just to let him get on with it

23 The same has been said of Ken Russell and Ridley Scott.
24 Except, apparently, on *Emmanuelle 5*.
25 Quoted in C. Tohill, 227.
26 Boro did fall out with some film producers, during films such as *Dr Jeckyll, The Art of Love* and *Emmanuelle 5*.

(film directors are well-known for not wanting to hear the word 'no' when they're filming. All they want to hear is, 'yes, I think we can do that' – preferrably with a 'sir' or a 'guv' added – or, in the case of some film directors, a cringing, terrified, whimpered, 'Yes, my master', uttered from a kneeling position).

I doubt there were extensive rehearsal periods for the actors, or any rehearsal at all.[27] Many Walerian Borowczyk scenes look as if the director has told an actor, 'OK, run along that path', 'How far?', 'I'll tell you when to stop'. And off they go.

Instead of explaining what he was after, Boro also showed them – by enacting the scene himself, gesture for gesture. Some actors loathe this approach, regarding it as demeaning, undermining their status as actors, and their abilities to interpret and invent.

So, no weeks of rehearsal prior to shooting, *à la* Robert Altman, D.W. Griffith or Francis Coppola. Which also means: no two-week 'Boro Camp,' where you learn how to run at speed while being chased by a monster thru dense undergrowth wearing nowt but a corset, and – sorry folks – no workshops for actors in 'Dildo Carving', 'Unlacing a Corset' or 'Masturbation With Rabbits'.

And a lot of Walerian Borowczyk's scenes look as if the scene was just one take, and Borowczyk would say fine, print, let's go to the next set-up, put the camera over here by the Renoir nude, Guy. I doubt that Borowczyk asked for endless takes like Michael Cimino, Jackie Chan or Stanley Kubrick – partly because these were low budget films, and precious film stock would need to be used carefully (and Boro liked to work fast). On the other hand, being a perfectionist would mean Borowczyk would likely keep going until it was close to being right. (Noël Véry has remarked that one reason for so many handheld shots in Boro's work was because, after preparing a scene meticulously, Boro liked to shoot rapidly. Some of the longer, intricate camera moves, though, would take time to light and rehearse).

---

27 However, some observers have said that some scenes were rehearsed.

But actors and crew kept coming back to the world of Walerian Borowczyk, which they wouldn't do if Boro was a dictator who was hell to work with. One reason was simple: you got to do stuff on a Borowczyk project, both in front of and behind the camera, that you seldom had the chance to do elsewhere. What the actors get up to in, say, *Immoral Tales* or *Behind Convent Walls*, is very different from a boring coffee commercial, or a day's walk-on part in a TV soap opera. And by the time of *Blanche* and *Immoral Tales*, Borowczyk had a certain reputation in film circles, which meant his films would be seen and discussed (no one wants to work on something that won't even be released, or will sink without trace). And working for Boro meant working for a genuine artistic talent, not a hack, a TV commercials director, or a director for hire. Boro was the real thing.

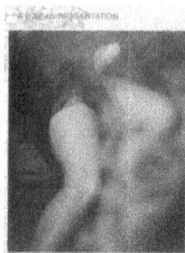

Love Rites
Directed by Walerian Borowczyk 18

the
Walerian Borowczyk
collection

THE BEAST   GOTO ISLAND OF LOVE   LOVE RITES

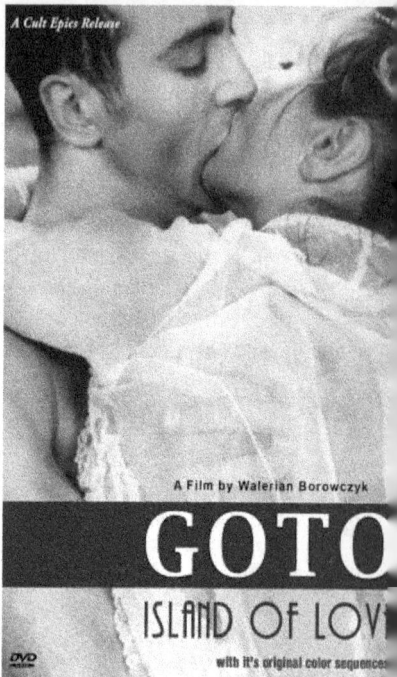

A Cult Epics Release

A Film by Walerian Borowczyk

GOTO
ISLAND OF LOVE

with it's original color sequences

Some artwork from releases of
Walerian Borowczyk's movies

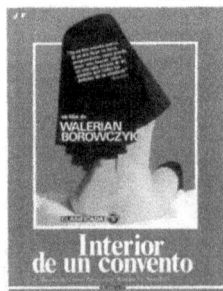

PHILOSOPH BOROWCZYK
Behind Convent Walls
INTÉRIEUR DE COUVENT
18

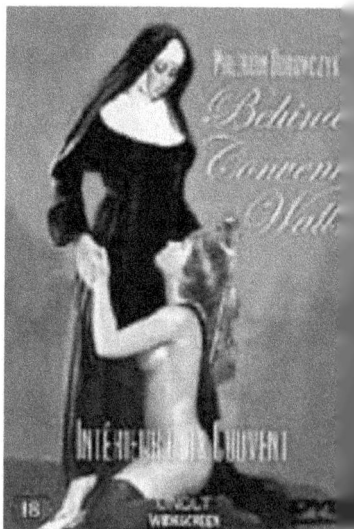

un film de
WALERIAN
BOROWCZYK

Interior
de un convento

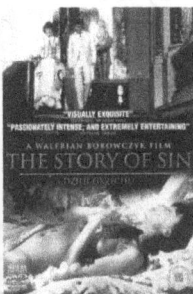

"VISUALLY EXQUISITE"
"PASSIONATELY INTENSE, AND EXTREMELY ENTERTAINING"

A WALERIAN BOROWCZYK FILM
THE STORY OF SIN

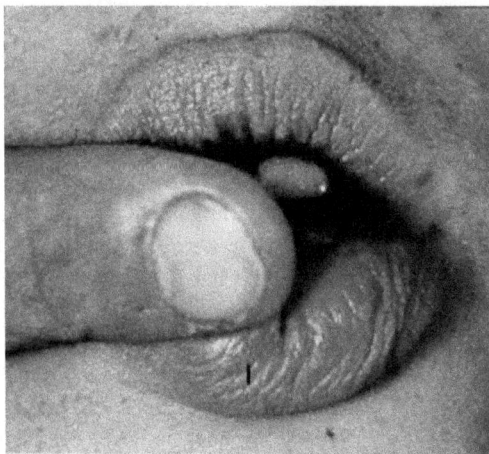

Contes immoraux

film de Walerian Borowczyk avec Paloma Picasso

RS AMANDI
L'arte di amare

You don't have to go to a museum to see an X-Rated Picasso

IMMORAL TALES

BOROWCZYK IN THE INTERNATIONAL MOVIE MARKET

Remember, too, that Walerian Borowczyk's films were low budget affairs. By low budget, I mean truly *low budget*. They were shot on 35mm film stock, true (and thankfully),[1] but Borowczyk would have been using (or been given) budgets in the region of, I reckon, $150,000-400,000, and maybe even less.[2] For a comparison, Hollywood calls a film 'low budget' these days if it's under millions of buck$ (say, $30m). However, Hollywood film budgets are not useful for comparisons, because everybody else in the world works with far less.

Another filmmaker working in La France, Jean-Luc Godard, produced films with budgets of typically $70,000, $90,000, $120,000 and $180,000 for his films thru the 1960s. *Aguirre, Wrath of God* (1972) was made, director Werner Herzog said, for $370,000 (and that was for an ambitious movie). The budget for *Last Tango in Paris* was $1.2 million (an Italian-French co-production, the money was North American, via United Artists[3]). The budget for *Derzu Uzala* (Akira Kurosawa, 1975) was in the region of $4,000,000. The budget of *Amarcord* (Federico Fellini, 1973) was $3.5 million.

It was the same with Walerian Borowczyk's contemporaries, like Pier Paolo Pasolini or Jean-Luc Godard: their financers and distributors knew that there was an audience for the films of these filmmakers within their country of origin. And if the subject matter was appealing (and nudity helped plenty as a marketing hook), the films might be able to travel outside of their country of origin. One must never forget that only a *tiny fraction* of films made in Europe get released in cinemas outside their country of origin – in the 1960s and 1970s

1 Because some 16mm footage from the 1960s and 1970s looks awful. However, some scenes of Boro's were filmed with 16mm – the tale in *The Beast*, for example, and the *Thérèse Philosophe* episode in *Immoral Tales*.
2 When deciding what to spend the budget on, you can bet that Borowczyk made sure the costumes on each film looked right. And they did.
3 The film was regarded as an Italian film being made on location in Paris.

as now (or even shown in a cinema *at all*). You may think 1,000s of foreign language movies are widely available, but there are many thousands more that don't travel beyond national borders. In other words, to get financed, the films must have been able to be sustained by the audiences of their own country (that is, Borowczyk's films were low budget partly because they would only be seen in a theatrical form predominantly in France or Italy).

Remember, too, that this was an era when ancillary markets were much smaller than today: no video, no DVD, no cable and satellite channels, no online outlets. Secondary markets of the 1960s-1970s would include television, film clubs, and not much else.[4] Only with the rise of home entertainment delivery systems in the Eighties would Walerian Borowczyk's films be able to generate revenue from areas outside of theatrical exhibition or television (and I bet quite a few of Borowczyk's films were rarely if ever shown on network TV).

But if we're talking about Walerian Borowczyk at all now, it means that his movies have had some life outside of their country of origin and their particular era. They have lived on, somehow. In itself, that's an amazing fact, because thousands of films and filmmakers have disappeared – from France, Italy, Spain, Germany, wherever in Europe, and will be remembered only by a few devotees. (Even fairly successful movies in the U.S.A. and Europe have almost completely disappeared. The greatest loss is from the silent cinema era: there are so many movies we would love to see. F.W.Murnau is a striking example: only half of the films of this mega-genius have survived).[5]

In all, Walerian Borowczyk directed 13 feature films

---

4 Specialist clubs, airlines, cruises and the rental of 16mm prints form other markets.
5 The lost Murnau movies include: *The Boy In Blue* (1919), *Satan* (1920), *The Hunchback and the Dancer* (1920), *Dr. Jekyll and Mr. Hyde* (1920), *Evening – Night – Morning* (1920), *Desire: The Tragedy of a Dancer* (1921), *Marizza, Called the Smuggler Madonna* (1922; one reel survives), *The Expulsion* (1923), and *Four Devils* (1928).

(and one TV film), and originated the ideas for some of them. Only later did Borowczyk become a director for hire, with producers coming to him with offers. It changes things considerably when you're developing projects yourself – you have much more of yourself invested in them, for a start (but they often take much longer to get going and to complete).

Hence the appeal of animation for Borowczyk – he could produce it with a tiny crew, or by himself (that is, *his* form of animation – other forms, such as full cel animation, or computer-aided animation, require larger crews and are massively labour-intensive). But everybody who works in animation knows this: it's a workaholics industry: *animation is hard work for little pay.*

Only 14 films (and you'll be doing well to see them all, too). We might lament that directors such as Donald Cammell, Stanley Kubrick or Andrei Tarkovsky didn't make many pictures, but at least all of them are readily available. But not Walerian Borowczyk, because he was making art before and after his feature film career. If you want to take in the *Collected Works* of Ingmar Bergman or Jean-Luc Godard, though, you're talking about huge amounts of film, video, television, radio and theatrical work. (And sourcing everything they've directed is a challenge).

(One wonders, though, what Walerian Borowczyk might have done with a mega budget, with the vast resources of set construction, location shooting, extras and visual effects of a contemporary blockbuster movie. It would never happen, of course, for numerous reasons. But a $200 million Borowczyk blockbuster movie is mind-boggling to contemplate!).

Another thing: thankfully, unlike some European art films one could mention, Walerian Borowczyk's films are 80 to 90 minutes long.[6] That's just right. No need for movies running two-and-a-half hours or more. No need for the misconceived length of *Céline and Julie Go Boating* or *The Damned* (*auteur* films which outlast their

[6] Incidentally, most were released in December, January or June.

welcome). Or contemporary Hollywood movies would often run to 2h 20m or more. Way, way, *way* too long. 2h 30m or more is OK for prestige pics like *Lawrence of Arabia* or *Schindler's List,* but not for junk like *Bad Boys 2* or a *Narnia* pic or *The Da Vinci Code.*

WALERIAN BOROWCZYK AND GENRE

Walerian Borowczyk stuck to particular genres in his films, and didn't venture into, say, gangster flicks, or science fiction, or Westerns, or musicals (a Borowczyk musical would be something to see!). Borowczyk is not interested in North America at all, such as so many of his European art film contemporaries, like Jean-Luc Godard, Wim Wenders or Rainer Werner Fassbinder. He doesn't quote from North American movies, doesn't use American stars in his films, and, crucially, isn't using American cinematic forms in his pictures. While filmmakers such as Godard were constantly critical of North America yet talked about American cinema, and admired it passionately, and recreated it in their films, Borowczyk just wasn't interested. (Not wholly true – Borowczyk's films *have* used American actors very occasionally: Joe Dallesandro in *The Streetwalker,* and the American actors in *Emmanuelle 5.* Also, there are U.S. characters in Boro's work – such as the American heiress Lucy in *The Beast*).

Walerian Borowczyk's movies remain resolutely *European,* the Old World not the New World, through and through (Werner Herzog and Ingmar Bergman resemble Borowczyk in this respect). There might have been overtures to Borowczyk from North American film producers or studios, but Borowczyk (like Pier Paolo Pasolini and Federico Fellini) preferred to remain in Europe to work. He didn't, like so many of his European contemporaries, 'go Hollywood' (and like so many

European filmmakers right back to the early days of cinema). And while filmmakers like Jean-Luc Godard or François Truffaut remained in Europe but used North American cinematic forms and ideas (and actors), Borowczyk never did. (However, he did work for some of the big names among European producers, such as Pierre Braunberger, Anatole Dauman, Alain Sarde, and the Hakim brothers – you will have seen movies by all of those producers).

And when we say that Walerian Borowczyk's movies are 'European', we also mean a very old idea of Europe. Borowczyk does deal with contemporary Europa, of course (not least with Communist Poland, his home country), and he does tackle the political and social situation in Europe from the 1950s onwards.[7] But, really, Borowczyk is interested in the idea of a Europe that stretches back into the 18th and 19th centuries, and into the Renaissance and the Middle Ages. And Borowczyk went right back to Ancient Rome, with his riff on the poet Ovid (in *The Art of Love*. Ovid was popular in the Middle Ages, in the courtly love tradition).

See, one of the most striking aspects of Walerian Borowczyk's cinema is that so many of his films were *historical*: they were costume dramas and historical movies (and his first feature film in live-action – for some his best film – *Goto: Island of Love* – was one of the strangest historical pictures ever made). That's a long tradition in the European art film, of course: every European art filmmaker has delved into history. But only a few have made historical films as their basic genre or type of movie.

There's Werner Herzog, and Pier Paolo Pasolini. And if European art filmmakers go back into the past, it's usually into the 20th century, and in particular the middle years – leading up to and during World War Two. Walerian Borowczyk, though, loves to explore older

7 Politics plays a huge part in Polish cinema, of course – and includes issues such as Communism, Solidarity, socialist realism, Marxism, liberalization, and continual confrontations and dialogues between the State and the film industry. Borowczyk, however, is not a typical Polish filmmaker – he's not a typical filmmaker in any respect!

cultures than that. And if he does do something set in the 20th century, it's the period *before* the First World War, before that catastrophe changed everything in Europe. (In this sense, Borowczyk's cinema is a perpetually *fin-de-siècle* cinema, always on the brink of collapse, always showing societies in decay).

Camille Paglia in *Sexual Personae* calls Hollywood the modern Rome, with its depictions of

> pagan sex and violence that have flowered so vividly in our mass media. The camera has unbound daemonic western imagination. Cinema is a *sexual showing*, a pagan flaunting. Plot and dialogue are obsolete word-baggage. Cinema, the most eye-intense of genres, has restored pagan antiquity's cultic exhibitionism. Spectacle is a pagan cult of the eye. (33)

❀

It's important, too, to remember that Walerian Borowczyk was an artist and animator for a long time before moving into live-action features. In other words, he wasn't only a filmmaker through-and-through, and wasn't a filmmaker throughout his artistic career. By the time *Goto: Island of Love* was released, for instance, Borowczyk was 46. His feature film career is actually a period of around twenty years, from 1967 to 1987 – and after that he continued to make art, write short stories and have exhibitions. (He also directed some TV, including *Série Rose*, in 1986 and 1990-1991.) Before and after his feature films, he produced short films, of course. (And he did commercial work, as even the greatest filmmakers have done, to make some $$$$).

One area of culture that Walerian Borowczyk seems perfectly suited to is directing opera – it fits with his passion for music, for design, for art direction, and for extravagant, historical visions. Several filmmakers of the 1980s and 1990s were invited to direct operas – Werner Herzog, Andrei Tarkovsky, Robert Altman, Ken Russell, etc.

Walerian Borowczyk said that whatever the medium

– film, short stories, painting – his creativity was the same. Jean-Luc Godard made similar remarks: filmmaking and writing were part of the same creative activity, and if he wasn't able to make movies, Godard said, he'd write. Woody Allen has often remarked that he'd be happy to write instead of directing. Borowczyk said he created very swiftly. 'I conceive all my films in an instant, and only objective means prevent me from making them in that instant' (D. Thomson, 2001). For Boro, cinema was simply another means of expression. It was just that, to produce feature movies, a team was required, considerable resources were needed – plus $$$$. (Also, several things have to come together to make a movie – groups of people, actors and schedules, the rights and options, studios and resources, the crew, etc. If one of the many factors aren't in place or ready, it can delay productions for years).

Which's why short films and animations appealed: Walerian Borowczyk could make them on his own, or with a few colleagues; he didn't have producers or financers breathing down his neck; he wasn't bound by ratings and many of the limitations/ conventions of commercial cinema; and consequently the subjects he chose to explore, and the way he explored them, could be much wider.

Clearly, Boro was an artist who enjoyed making things – be it bizarre props for his movies, or posters, or short animated pieces, or graphic art. And thus the *handmade* aspect of making art/ cinema was valorized – not having everything smoothed-out and clean, not adhering to perfect proportions and lines, allowing for spontaneity and accidents, and enjoying the *process* of making art.

❈

I've mentioned how exotic and weird Walerian Borowczyk's films are, but there were many pictures made in the 1960s and 1970s which were just as crazy – I mean those movies labelled 'mondo cinema', or 'exploitation cinema', or 'sexploitation', or '*fantastique* cinema*', or 'underground cinema'. And spoofing Catholic themes and imagery is a big part of those European movies (understandable, being as many were made in and for Italy, France and Spain). There are films about vampires, Dracula, Frankenstein, monsters, occultism, horror, nuns, Satanism, the Devil, cannibals, zombies, ghosts, serial killers, and on and on, in 100s of films made in Europe from the 1960s to the 1980s, the era when Borowczyk was active in feature filmmaking.

And Walerian Borowczyk's flicks, with their eroticized nuns, their sex scenes and nudity, their sense of the grotesque, their explosions of violence and blood, are very much part of low budget, European filmmaking of the 1960s-80s, part of the cast of horror, sex, *mondo*, exploitation and *fantastique* films – the vampires, aliens, serial killers, babes and freaks. (And Hollywood and North American TV of course recycles vampires and horror numerous times – the *Vampire Diaries, Underworld, True Blood* and the *Twilight* movie and TV franchises being recent vampiric examples).

Part of the reason is that horror, thriller and occult films are cheap to make (a guy in a mask, a big knife, and a screaming girl, filmed in existing, contemporary settings). And that's also why so many of those movies include nudity – all you have to do is get people to take off their clothes; nudity and sex are among the cheapest effects in cinema, and they're guaranteed to get attention. You don't have to build vast sets or have costly costumes. It's the same with porno films (and also why porn often takes up horror or sci-fi or occult genres). As low budget, Spanish horror maestro José Larraz put it:

> When you have no money, the only guarantee for the box office is sex. How can I make a film like *The Spy Who Came In From the Cold* with inexperienced actors and no money?[8]

So although we exalt filmmakers such as Walerian Borowczyk or Werner Herzog or Sergei Paradjanov or Pier Paolo Pasolini or whoever – because they are 'serious' filmmakers, filmmakers who've made some

8 Quoted in C. Tohill, 199.

'serious' work which can be properly called 'art' – there are hundreds of other filmmakers and films of that period which contain just as much outrageous imagery. I mean filmmakers like José Bénazéraf, Jess Franco, Jean Rollin, José Larraz, Massimo Pupillo, Mario Bava, etc. Or maybe it's because, somehow, filmmakers like Pasolini, Alain Robbe-Grillet and Borowczyk have survived, while so many others have been forgotten.

MOTIFS AND THEMES

A list of the motifs and tropes appearing in Boro's films would include:
- funerals and coffins;
- meat and carcasses (and blood);
- horses (they appear in many Borowczyk movies);
- self-contained communities;
- flowers (typically roses, including their thorns);
- fruit (arranged in still-life images);
- statues and busts;
- flies;
- dogs;
- erotic books and prints;
- Catholic iconography;
- churches;
- confessions and confessionals;
- baths and bathing (usually women);
- phallic substitutes;
- mediæval and Renaissance paintings and art;
- naked bodies;
- female masturbation;
- pre-modern keyboards;
- music (typically organ or harpsichord, 18th and 19th centuries).

And the themes in Boro's cinema include: suicide; corruption; exploitation; female *jouissance*; death;

religion; sin; voyeurism; the role of the artist in modern society (including artists and models); the relation between individuals and societies; love and romance (relationships are often vaguely sadomasochistic); prostitution, and so on.

Dolls, puppets, statues and busts are further motifs in Boro's cinema (animators absolutely adore puppets and dolls, and automata and robots, for obvious reasons, such as the evocation of intermediary states of existence between flesh-and-blood humans and inanimate objects).

Animators love dogs – probably more than any other animal. So maybe it's no surprise that pooches run and bark through many Borowczyk films, including *Blanche, Goto, The Beast* and *Three Immoral Women.* (The doggie in the 'Marie' episode in *Three Immoral Women* is a Hound of Hell, attacking and punishing the two men in the heroine's life – her kidnapper and husband).

SERIAL KILLERS.

That death is one of Walerian Borowczyk's chief concerns goes without saying. I mean, it's a key issue in pretty much every major filmmaker in film history (and certainly in *all* of the important European directors of the postwar period). But Boro's cinema also focusses on murder and murderers: from *Goto* onwards, serial killers stalk through a striking proportion of Borowczyk's output: Countess Báthory in *Immoral Tales,* Jack the Ripper in *Lulu,* Dr Jeckyll/ Mr Hyde in *The Strange Case of Dr. Jeckyll and Miss Osbourne* and 'La Fornarina' in *Three Immoral Women* (and Marceline kills her parents). Plus, Boro was planning a film about Gilles de Rais.

Not as many killers as Alfred Hitchcock, then, compared to his 50+ movies – but, in terms of the smaller amount of flicks helmed by Boro (13 features), it's a significant amount of mass murder.

One can easily discern the influence of Walerian Borowczyk on filmmakers – partly because his vision is so distinctive (and sensual), and also because he is very much a filmmaker's filmmaker, a film director who celebrates the construction of cinema, the Mélièsian tricks and the sleights of hand of cinema – and the sheer joy of making cinema. Borowczyk's influence can be seen in filmmakers such as David Lynch (*Eraserhead,* 1978, and *The Elephant Man,* 1980), Andrei Tarkovsky (*Mirror,* 1974, and *Stalker,*9 1979), Terry Gilliam (*Jabberwocky,* 1977, and the *Monty Python* animations), Luc Besson (*The Last Battle*, 1984), and Jeunet and Caro (the latters' films *Delicatessen* (1991) and *The City of Lost Children* (1995) contain references to Borowczyk's *Goto: Island of Love.* Indeed, *The City of Lost Children* is a virtual remake of *Goto* in many respects, down to the humour, the surreal imagery, and the stylized, shabby wood, metal and stone *mise-en-scène.* Boro was doing steam-punk years before it became cool).

Terry Gilliam said he and fellow *Monty Python* Terry Jones loved Borowczyk's *Goto: Island of Love* and *Blanche.* Of Borowczyk's short *Jeux des anges,* Gilliam said it was

> just extraordinary: the sense that you're on a train with the walls of the city going past, and then the sound of angels' wings – incredible... Terry Jones and I went crazy over Borowczyk because his films were so much about atmosphere and texture. (T. Gilliam, 39)

As well as Terry Gilliam, the Quay Brothers (*Street of Crocodiles*), Catherine Breillat and Neil Jordan10 have expressed their admiration for Walerian Borowczyk. Borowczyk has his fans among critics – such as Ado

9 *Stalker* is thoroughly Borowczykian.
10 Jordan had a go at his own version of an erotic, Freudian update of a Grimm fairy tale in *Company of Wolves* (1984), but although it's fêted in British film critical circles, *The Company of Wolves* isn't a patch on a Borowczyk movie.

Kryou, David Thomson, Tom Milne, and Mark Kermode.

WALERIAN BOROWCZYK AND EROTICISM

Walerian Borowczyk's is a highly cultured cinema, a cinema of (and for) connoisseurs – eclectic, subtle, mysterious and haunting. Many films were based on literary sources: Ovid (*Art of Love*), André Pieyre de Mandiargues (*The Streetwalker, Immoral Tales, Three Immoral Women* and *Love Rites*), Robert Louis Stevenson (*Dr Jeckyll*), Franz Wedekind (*Lulu*), and Stendhal[11] (*Behind Convent Walls*). Borowczyk certainly delivered on one count: there was plenty of nudity, plenty of sex, but his films were also that rare thing, *erotic*.

Walerian Borowczyk claimed that the sexual component in his cinema had been over-emphasized – that's partly because *he* over-emphasizes it and *his films* over-emphasize it! He was a film director who included scenes of (to use the technical/ medical terms): incest, fellatio, cunnilingus, intercourse, lesbianism, pederasty, pædophilia, bondage, sadomasochism, etc. (He also claimed his films weren't erotic, and his supporters also claim that – eroticism was just another part of life).

Were there ever so many movies of one director so in love with women's torsos, bellies, hips, buttocks, thighs and vulvas? Walerian Borowczyk's work delights in medium close-ups of women's bodies, framed from the thighs to the belly. He has them turn this way and that, sometimes naked, sometimes draped with gauzy material, sometimes with the light shining from behind, sometimes in flat light, sometimes in soft focus. (As director Jess Franco remarked, 'it's the first thing I look at').

These shots go beyond softcore porn, or mere titillation, as detractors call them; they become painterly appreciations of form, shape, tone, colour. They recall

11 Sort of, but not really.

sculptors such as Eric Gill, Aristide Maillol and Auguste Rodin, sculptors who worshipped that part of the female form in bronze and marble. Walerian Borowczyk's films' endless images of women's bodies concentrating on the torso, buttocks and hips also recall 19th century nude paintings by Gustave Moreau, Jean Auguste Dominique Ingres or Gustave Courbet, or the thousands of art academy nudes (in the 19th century, painting female nudes became a virtual industry. Indeed, every major art museum on the planet today contains female nude paintings, and many of them were made in the 1800s).

Women bathing is a legitimate reason for depicting women naked – because they're bathing, right? Hence, in 19th century academy art, women were portrayed taking baths – such as in the seraglios in the art of Jean Auguste Dominique Ingres and later painters such as Lawrence Alma-Tadema and Lord Leighton. And earlier, Renaissance artists such as Titian and Tintoretto painted Goddesses taking a bath (such as Venus), or Bathsheba from the *Bible*. The numerous scenes of women bathing in Borowczyk's cinema are part of this tradition. You could piece together an exhibition of stills from Borowczyk's movies solely of naked women bathing.

Walerian Borowczyk certainly knows his history of religion and sex, the links between spirit and flesh; the Passion and pornography; extreme religious faith and erotic fervour; mysticism and masturbation. Among the 20th century artists who've addressed the fusion between sex and spirit are Georges Bataille, D.H. Lawrence, James Joyce, John Cowper Powys, Eric Gill, and directors such as Luis Buñuel, Ingmar Bergman and Pier Paolo Pasolini. (There are numerous links between the works of Buñuel and Borowczyk – both come from the same sort of intellectual, Surrealist, European tradition. Parts of Buñuel's wonderful autobiography *My Last Sigh* read like a Borowczyk film. However, when it comes to the satirical criticism of Catholicism and Christianity, which Buñuel is known for, I reckon Borowczyk's take was superior.)

Walerian Borowczyk is certainly very much in the

same tradition of *avant garde* and modernist, European literature that explores sexual and religious issues in extreme manifestations: Borowczyk is part of the tradition which includes Surrealists like Hans Bellmer[12] with his dolls photographed in erotic scenarios, with fingers penetrating orifices; or Georges Bataille with his pornography of eyes, eggs, asses and mouths in *The Story of the Eye* (an influential but much over-rated novella);[13] or the dreamscapes of arch Surrealist prankster Salvador Dali; or the far superior Surrealism of Luis Buñuel; or the man behind it all in France: the Marquis de Sade. And those writers who were just as extreme, and still part of that 'no limits', modernist tradition: Henry Miller, Pauline Réage, Jean de Berg, Emmanuelle Arsan, William Burroughs, D.H. Lawrence, Anaïs Nin, etc.

There is also a fashionable, European (and very 'French') fascination with sodomy and the anus among these writers and filmmakers: it's found in the works of writers[14] such as the Marquis de Sade, Jean Genet, Georges Bataille (*The Story of the Eye*), William Burroughs (*The Naked Lunch*), Marco Vassi, D.H. Lawrence (*Lady Chatterley's Lover*), Henry Miller (*The Rosy Crucifixion*) and the Surrealists,[15] in artists such as Pierro Mazoni (who sold cans of his turds for their weight in gold in 1962), and Pierre Louÿs[16] (one of Louÿs' books was a study of women's asses, entitled *La cul de la femme*, which might appear as a prop in a Boro movie), and in films such as *Last Tango in Paris, Weekend, Le Grande Bouffe* and *Ai No Corrida*.

Walerian Borowczyk maintained that he wasn't a

---

12 Borowczyk included a Bellmeresque drawing in *The Beast*, which he drew.
13 *The Story of the Eye* and Georges Bataille are favourites with the Euro intelligentsia and filmmakers (such as Jean-Luc Godard).
14 There are connections made between the anal and the spiritual, materialism and mysticism ('excremental' mysticism) in the fiction of authors such as Henry Miller, D.H. Lawrence, James Joyce and John Cowper Powys.
15 As in Salvador Dali's *Virgin Autosodomized By Her Own Chastity*.
16 Pierre Louÿs (1870-1925) has affinities with Boro. He wrote erotic fiction, and also took lots of erotic photographs.

maker of erotic films, and disliked that kind of categorization. It was too narrow, for a start, and was more to do with how people perceived him and his films, than who he really was, or what his movies really were. Besides, Borowczyk said, sex was no more unusual than eating or smoking cigarettes. When an interviewer called him a pervert, he replied, 'who isn't a pervert?' Everyone's interested in sex, Borowczyk alleged, and it was as fundamental to being alive as eating, drinking, sleeping or anything else.

When you look closer, you can see that Walerian Borowczyk's films aren't particularly pervy – especially when compared to many strands of pornography. Even Borowczyk's most controversial production as director, *The Beast*, depicts heterosexual sex (apart from the Curé and his choirboys, which's not really shown). And everything the Beast does with Romilda is within the bounds of regular heterosexual sex (aside from the rape aspect). Indeed, there are depictions of sex in mainstream films which are much more 'perverse' than the sex in *The Beast*. And pictures such as *Ai No Corrida* (*In the Realm of the Senses*, 1976)[17] are way more perverse and objectionable (if you want to see them like that), than the sex in *The Beast* (in *Ai No Corrida* the lovers literally fuck themselves to death!).

(Side-note: But, wait, it is true that the sex in *The Beast* is between a woman and (what is meant to be/ taken to be) a monster! And there is coercion and rape in *The Beast*. And you couldn't really use *The Beast* as an example in an argument for promoting nice, normal intercourse in a safe, consensual relationship among cosy, middle-class Christians!).

'Desire' is perhaps a better term than sex or eroticism – 'desire' with all its philosophical associations with the Lacanian lack, with loss, and with distance (a key component of voyeurism). The looking and looked-at-ness in Borowczyk's cinema emphasizes the sadness and loss of the distances between people. Looking is not always pleasurable in Borowczyk's work – the observers

17 Produced by Anatole Dauman, Borowczyk's producer.

are not always getting off on peeping: rather, looking reminds them of their own loneliness, their separateness from everything.[18] (Instead of voyeurism or scopophilia, psychological terms used by Sigmund Freud and Walter Benjamin, maybe *Schaulust* is better, the German term for 'lust of the eyes', or rubber-necking, Karin Littau suggested in an essay on early cinema[19]).

Walerian Borowczyk defended his films by saying:

all I do is express everyone's dreams.

'I think we filmmakers often find ourselves trying to fill up the missing something of the audience's emotions and psychological needs', director Tsui Hark remarked. It was odd, wasn't it, Boro maintained, that critics always talked about him, rather than the thousands of viewers and consumers who watched his movies. Borowczyk resisted that biographical approach of most film criticism, which always relates films to the filmmakers, which always says that *Citizen Kane* is ultimately about Orson Welles (even more than about William Randolph Hearst or similar business tycoons). By that token, Borowczyk asserted, if you make films or stories about serial killers, you risked being branded as a serial killer yourself. It was all very silly, and Boro clearly grew tired of people making the same assumptions about him time after time.

18 Pier Paolo Pasolini made a remark of sex in cinema that resonates here, how seeing sex emphasizes sadness and distance.
19 In J. Geiger, 58.

WALERIAN BOROWCZYK AND ANDRÉ DE MANDIARGUES

André Pieyre de Mandiargues (Mch 14, 1909 – Paris - Dec 13, 1991) is an important figure among Walerian Borowczyk's collaborators: he provided the stories for *La Marge, Love Rites,* parts of *Immoral Tales* and *Three Immoral Women,* and the narration, props and much of *Une Collection particulière.* Altho' he was 14 years older, de Mandiargues shared a similar outlook on life with Boro (and also the same sense of humour). De Mandiargues also wrote the 1963 novel that was the basis for the movie *Girl On a Motorcycle* (a.k.a. *Naked Under Leather,* dir. Jack Cardiff, 1968). Aside from *Girl On a Motorcycle* and Borowczyk's films,[20] no one else seems to have produced movies from de Mandiargues' fiction.

André Pieyre de Mandiargues was linked to the Surrealist movement (he was friends with Leonor Fini, and thru her, other Surrealists). Among de Mandiargues' literary works were: *Le Musée noir* (1946), *L'Anglais décrit dans le château fermé* (1953), *Le Lis de mer* (1956), *Le Belvédère* (1958), *Feu de braise* (1959, as *Blaze of Embers,* 1971), *La Motocyclette* (*The Motorcycle,* 1963), *La Marge* (1967, as *The Margin,* 1970), *Isabella Morra* (1974) and *Tout Disparaîtra* (*Everything Must Go,* 1987). He also wrote an introduction for *The Story of O* (in 1958).

---

20 One of Borowczyk's short films, *Esgarot de Venus* (1975), was a document of the art of Mandiargues' wife, Bona Tibertelli De Pisis. It's a minor work in the Boro canon, partly because De Pisis's erotic art isn't very inspiring.

SOME OF WALERIAN BOROWCZYK'S
INFLUENCES

Walerian Borowczyk lived in Paris for much of his life; Paris seemed to be a favourite destination for Eastern European and Polish filmmakers – Roman Polanski and Krzysztof Kieslowski ended up there (some directors, like Andrej Wadja, remained in Poland). And many other filmmakers gravitated towards Paris and France: Luis Buñuel, Raul Ruiz and Pedro Almodóvar. Why Paris? One reason is that France has one of the strongest film cultures in the world: France produces more films than any nation in Europe (there is more State support for cinema than many other places), there are good resources, crews, actors[21] and studios there, and people go to the cinema more in France than anywhere in Europa. It's an excellent place to make films (and Paris itself photographs like a dream).[22]

Aspects of French art in particular have long been interested (even obsessed) with sexuality and (Catholic) religion: Gustave Moreau, Félicien Rops, J.-K. Huysmans, Gustave Flaubert, Odilon Redon, Jean Delville, and the whole *fin-de-siècle* Symbolist and Decadent æsthetic movements. (Consider Rops' riotous, blasphemous images of Satan, devils, phalluses and naked women).

Walerian Borowczyk's sensuous, intellectual art cinema is clearly informed by the history of high European culture that goes back through the modernist *avant garde* and Surrealism (1920s/ 30s), via Symbolism and *fin-de-siècle* Decadence (1880s/ 90s), to the Romantics (1780s/1830s), to the Marquis de Sade (late 1700s) and 18th century pornography, and further back, via Renaissance painting (1400s/ 1600s), to the flamboyance and debauchery of the Medicis, the Borgias and Catherine the Great. Thence to mediæval religion and art (monasteries and convents, and the highpoint of Catholic art), bypassing the Dark Ages, to Ancient Greek and Roman times.

21 There are wonderful actors and extras in Paris.
22 And most of Boro's movies were made in French, his second language. And with mainly French crews.

One could analyze Walerian Borowczyk's cinema in relation to any of those eras and cultural movements. The affinities between Borowczyk's films and the Symbolist and Decadent age are obvious. For instance, *fin-de-siècle* 'high' culture was marked by 'gory exoticism', as Mario Praz put it in *The Romantic Agony* (289), by mysticism and black magic, occultism, Satanism, Catholic imagery, the macabre, the æstheticism of 'beauty', a love of costumes, dressing up, cross-dressing and dandyism, an attraction to Oriental and Byzantine culture, opulence and indulgence, where the key phrase is from Paul Verlaine: 'Je suis l'Empire à la fin de la décadence', as Verlaine wrote in 1885 in his poem 'Langueur' (1974, 180).

The age was summed up by works of literature such as Arthur Rimbaud's *Une Saison en Enfer*, Comte de Lautréamont's *Chansons de Maldoror*, Edgar Allan Poe's horror stories, Charles Baudelaire's *Flowers of Evil*, Gustave Flaubert's *Salambô* and *La Tentation de saint Antoine*, J.-K. Huysmans' *À Rebours* and *Là-bas*, Bram Stoker's *Dracula*, Joséphin Péladan's *Le Vice suprême*, and music such as Richard Wagner's *Parsifal*. (Some of the key artists of the Decadent and Symbolist epoch, apart from the writers and painters noted above, included Honoré de Balzac, Jean Moréas, Albert Aurier, Octave Mirabeau, Walter Pater, Jan Troop, Oscar Wilde, Pierre Louÿs, Arnold Böcklin, Puvis de Chavannes and Stéphane Mallarmé.) Borowczyk is wholly at home in this cultural *milieu*, and draws on it.

Walerian Borowczyk is a devotee of Surrealism, too – and Surrealism's preoccupation with sex and death, and with cruelty and absurdity, is an important element in his cinema. 'Beauty will be convulsive, or not all,' remarked the godfather of Surrealism, André Breton, and that's Borowczyk's maxim too. (And it's Surrealism as informed by the psychoanalysis of Sigmund Freud; Boro, born in 1923, is a product culturally of the mid-century, when Freudianism and psychoanalysis were at the height of their popularity).

Walerian Borowczyk also has the Surrealists' love of

bizarre objects, and his cinema is full of them – from the fly-catching box in *Goto: Island of Love* to the metal finger extensions of the hooker in *Love Rites*. (The fly-catching box, with its funnels ending in dog's hair, is a classic Surrealist device – it could be part of an exhibition by Max Ernst or Marcel Duchamp, and it looks forward to contemporary artists such as Rebecca Horn). And Borowczyk also employs Surrealism's use of juxtaposition: put two apparently innocuous objects together to form a third, strange being.[23] (Boro's editing style delivers many such poetic collisions).

Walerian Borowczyk is also fond of secret objects, objects that are hidden and have to be revealed – taken out of cabinets, or unfolded, or found at the bottom of a trunk of clothes. In *La Bête* there's a family album with pages that are unfolded to reveal erotic drawings, and when a framed text is reversed it reveals a sketch of a horse coupling with a woman.

Then there's the emphasis in Surrealism on dreams, on dream imagery, on the unconscious, *à la* Sigmund Freud or C.G. Jung *et al*. Walerian Borowczyk called *Immoral Tales* 'a sanctuary for liberty, an island of no restrictions': he has the 'no limits' philosophy of the Surrealists and the *avant garde* in Europe of the 20th century. 'All I do is express everyone's dreams', Borowczyk insisted: he was simply filming what everybody was dreaming about.

Carl Jung wrote:

> The cinema, like the detective story, makes it possible to experience without danger all the excitement, passion and desirousness which must be suppressed in a humanitarian ordering of society.

Linked to Surrealism is the Existentialist philosophy in Walerian Borowczyk's cinema: he is definitely a figure of the mid-to-late 20th century (or his artistic and

23 Of painters, Borowczyk said he was impressed by Tomasso Capelli, a 14th century Italian painter, Henri Lecourbe, and his own father (J. Gerber, 171). Among Polish painters, Borowczyk admired Piotr Michalowsky (d. 1855) and Tadeusz Makowski (d. 1932).

political views seem to have been formed partly by the debates in Existentialism of the mid-century: he was a teenager between 1936 and 1943 – his youth occurred in the run-up to WWII and throughout the war). There are also correspondences between Borowczyk's cinema and the Theatre of the Absurd of Samuel Beckett, Antonin Artaud and Eugène Ionesco. Part of that Existential belief is expressed in the cruelty and absurdity of modern life in Borowczyk's *œuvre*. It's a view that encompasses pessimism, irony, and detachment. A view that sees the horrors of modern life and decides that not a lot can assuage them (hence the black humour and irony, as a defence against the overwhelming horrors of the mid-20th century).

David Cook in *A History of Narrative Film* writes:

> From both his live-action features and his animated films, it is clear that Borowczyk shares with many of his compatriots a fatalistic and absurdist vision of life. His work embodies a profound pessimism for the human heritage of dissolution, disorder, and decay. But pessimism is not cynicism and need not lead to despair. There is in Borowczyk's films a kind of affirmation in his utter outrage at human misery and in his sense of horror at the human stupidities that produce it. (678-9)

Decline and fall is the fundamental narrative trajectory of all of Borowczyk's long films, pretty much (and many of the short films gravitate towards entropy). From *Goto* to *Love Rites*, nearly all of them depict things falling apart, a descent into chaos, ending in death. Several movies end in hysterical, apocalyptic chaos (*The Beast, Behind Convent Walls, Dr Jeckyll*), and most of the others close with deaths (*The Art of Love, Blanche, Goto, Immoral Tales, Three Immoral Women, Lulu, The Story of Sin* and *The Streetwalker*).

The politics of Walerian Borowczyk's cinema ranges from the expected left-liberal politics of Parisian intellectuals and artists (and artists living in exile from Poland and Communist regimes), to the conservative, right-wing politics of many of the stories, the characters and the issues his cinema explores. That is, altho' Boro's origins might've been in experimental animation, with nods to the European *avant garde*, and in art history and the history of painting, much of his cinema is actually dealing with traditional, conservative and even right-wing issues/ characters/ stories.

Meanwhile, horror/ fantasy cinema is predominantly right-wing and conservative, despite its apparent radical critiques of societies, its examination/ over-turning of social norms and *mœurs*, its libertarian project, and its rebel status within cinema as a whole. (Which's one reason why conservative film industries such as Hollywood churn out fantasy and horror by the ton).

The view among some who deride Borowczyk's erotic-romantic films is: why, at a time of the tumultuous political events in Poland in the early 1980s, was Borowczyk squandering his immense talents in directing *The Art of Love* or *Emmanuelle 5*? While his Polish contemporaries tackled contemporary political issues, Solidarity and State oppression, Borowczyk and his entourage were retreating to Ancient Rome (and not, either, to deliver a scathing attack on the political establishment, using Ancient Roman politics as an analogy or metaphor, but to loon about with bored housewives taking baths).

However, a view like that is filled with assumptions – about what a filmmaker is, what they do, and how they operate. It also ignores Boro's other work, such as his short films and artworks (where his political critique is certainly angrier, and *Dr Jeckyll* is a very angry film).

One of Walerian Borowczyk's notions was that Walt Disney's films were more pornographic than his own (one imagines what the studio executives at the Walt Disney Studios in Burbank, viewing a DVD of *The Beast* or *Immoral Tales* beside their own *Aladdin* or *Bambi*, would make of that idea!). Borowczyk said that *Snow White and the Seven Dwarfs* was much more erotic than any of his own films because of its 'stench of unsatisfied desire'. (Boro displayed the Euro artist's distrust and dislike of

Disney (with anti-Americanism as part of it) – perhaps, I would imagine, because he would get weary of questions about Disney in reference to animation, and his own work in animation. Because Disney still tends to be the first thing people think of when cartoons and animation are mentioned. Every animator gets asked about Disney, and they weary of it. The Disney corporation has colonized animation in cinema, and there are thousands of rebels)[24]

Asked who he'd like to be in history if he had the choice, Walerian Borowczyk said: 'if I have to choose an epoch and an identity, it would be that of Leda's swan in antiquity (if she really was as beautiful as the artists represent her)' (J. Gerber, 172-3). The greatest representation of Leda is of course Leonardo da Vinci's lost painting – a copy gives some idea of the beauty of Leda.[25] There's also a lost version by Michelangelo Buonarroti, which's even more explicit: the giant swan lies between the woman's legs, its wing covering her vulva.[26] Both are known from copies[27]

That is typical of Walerian Borowczyk's eccentricity – to be the swan that makes love to Leda. But the swan was of course a god – Jupiter – in disguise.

24 Animators, already fed up with that, also dislike the notion that what they do is 'anti-Disney', or perpetually in relation to Disney.
25 Leonardo's *Leda* was burned by Madame de Maintenon around 1700, or was destroyed by one of Louis XIII's henchmen.
26 There's a copy of *Leda and the Swan*, 16th century, in London's Royal Academy.
27 Anonymous, the 'ex-Spiridon version', *Leda and the Swan*, wood, 132 x 78cm, Rome; anonymous: *Leda and the Swan*, 112 x 86cm, Galleria Borghese, Rome.

My friend, sensual pleasure was always the dearest
of my possessions. I have worshipped it all my life
and I wish to embrace it to my end.

Marquis de Sade, *Dialogue entre un Prêtre et un
Moribond* (1782)

God of the Surrealists, of French intellectuals and
bohemians, and the Grand Emperor of Pornographers,
and wannabe trendies and avant gardists, Donatien-
Alphonse-François de Sade, a.k.a. the Marquis de Sade
(1740-1814), is the controversial author of 4 novels, short
stories, plays, dialogues, letters, journals and pamphlets
(including *Justine, Philosophy of the Bedroom, The
Story of Juliette* and *Les Cent Vingt Journés de
Sodome*). De Sade's was a notorious life, leading to a
number of spells in prison (prostitutes, attempts on his
life, run-ins with the police, accused of poisoning
Marseilles hookers, etc)[28] He apparently indulged in some
of the sadomasochistic practices described in his fiction
(some of which led to his imprisonment); that's part of
the Sadean Legend, of course.[29]

The Marquis de Sade has been exalted to the status
of Major Philosopher for many Euro-intellectuals, taking
his place alongside Friedrich Nietzsche, Sigmund Freud,
Karl Marx and Jean-Paul Sartre. De Sade is a perfect
author for filmmakers such as Pier Paolo Pasolini, Jean-
Luc Godard, Rainer Maria Fassbinder, Luis Buñuel and
Walerian Borowczyk.

The 120 Days of Sodom was written while the
Marquis de Sade was in prison. It is set shortly before
1715. As Margaret Crosland describes in her excellent *de
Sade Reader, The 120 Days of Sodom* came directly out

28 According to Gérard Zwang, 'it is because of excessive
imprisonment and vindictive and cowardly censorship that Sade
has been put on a pedestal and consecrated a martyr, great
philosopher, major writer and specialist in eroticism' (quoted in
B. Groult: "Les portiers de nuit", in *Ainsi soit-elle*, Grasset,
Paris, 1975, and in E. Marks, 69).
29 We want to believe that notorious writers are *really* notorious! And not like everybody else.

of de Sade's experience of being behind bars:

> If his physical life was empty, his head was full of
> ideas. He now began to write the blackest of his
> books; blackest because no ray of light, no memory
> of what might have been happy or 'good' ever
> gleams through it. Sade conceived and wrote it (part
> of it, at least) as though the 'normal' world did not
> exist, and he may well have thought that even if it
> did, he might never see it again. (2000, 31)

The Marquis de Sade also possessed the childish
urge to shock society – in common with the Surrealists
and so many other avant gardists (and a good many
filmmakers, too!). There is undoubtedly a yen to startle
audiences, a conscious effort to find *something* that will
annoy someone in the audience. After de Sade, the
fiction of Henry Miller, Jean Genet, Georges Bataille and
William Burroughs seems a mere postscript. This extract
from *The 120 Days of Sodom* is typical:

> Curval, who had not been experiencing such an
> onslaught, blasphemed with joy. He quivered in
> excitement, opened his legs wide and prepared
> himself. At that moment the youthful sperm of the
> charming boy he was masturbating dripped down to
> the enormous tip of his frenzied instrument. This
> warm sperm which drenched him, the repeated
> shuddering of the duke who was beginning to
> discharge also, everything led him on, everything
> brought on his climax and floods of foaming sperm
> flooded Durcet's arse.[30]

The Marquis de Sade has been a high profile and
much-loathed target for feminists. Andrea Dworkin
decimated de Sade in her 1983 book *Pornography*. 'The
commercialized sex movement's theoreticians have
unearthed the Marquis de Sade and undertaken to deify
him', noted Benoîte Groult (ib., 69).
And the Marquis de Sade himself has been the
subject of many movies and famous plays, including the
play *Marat/ Sade,* horror flicks from Jess Franco and

30 Quoted in M. Crosland, 2000, 37.

Hammer horror (with the Marquis as a villain or monster), to lit'ry, arty fare such as the play and film *Quills* (2000). Richard Matheson, Peter Brook, Tobe Hooper, Luis Buñuel, Phillip Kaufman, Jan Svankmajer and others have taken on de Sade as a person or character, and he's been played by Klaus Kinski, Christopher Lee, Geoffrey Rush, Keir Dullea, Patrick Magee, Robert Englund and Daniel Auteuil. (De Sade also appears in *Softly From Paris*, dir. by Borowcyk, tho' not as a lecherous monster).

WALERIAN BOROWCZYK'S VISUALS AND STYLE

Walerian Borowczyk has no superior when it comes to art direction in cinema. I reckon his art direction is the equal of celebrated examples, such as Cedric Gibbons and the M.G.M. unit (regarded with religious awe by *cinéastes*), or Walter Roehrig, Walter Reimann and Hermann Warm, who did the settings for *The Cabinet of Dr Caligari*. Is Borowczyk that good? Yes, I think he is (tho' his works are not as well-known). He goes beyond creating a complete and convincing world and settings which serve the story and the film.

Walerian Borowczyk has the credits of editor and production designer on many of his films. Many of the props and designs in Borowczyk's cinema have an appealing, handmade feel to them, and Borowczyk himself created some of them. You could mount an exhibition of the props in Borowczyk's films and it would be a great show (and more interesting than some other film exhibitions which are often disappointing, as if cinema, which only exists on TV monitors and screens, as projections, is not as compelling as objects or things are). A filmmaker such as Jan Svankmajer and Sergei Paradjanov had a similar handmade, earthy feel to their props. In Borowczyk's cinema, it's the classic eroticization of the object – the (art) object as fetish.

Walerian Borowczyk was particularly fond of a frontal, *tableau* approach to staging and blocking scenes, filmng scenes against a single wall. The approach isn't interested in creating simulations of three-dimensional space (by moving the camera, for example, around the actors, or from the side). Instead, it's a pictorial style, flattening (and mergining) foreground and background, and drawing on pre-Renaissance art.

The *tableau* approach is found also in, for example, the cinema of Pier Paolo Pasolini (in Pasolini's work, it partly derived from the flattened space of 14th and 15th century Renaissance art). Carl-Theodor Dreyer often used the *tableau* style – in *Ordet* (1955), for instance.[31] Sergei Paradjanov was a master of the form – in *The Shadows of Our Forgotten Ancestors* (1964) and *The Color of Pomegranates* (1969). Theo Angelopoulos took it up in films like *Ulysses' Gaze* (1995). Werner Herzog exploited the *tableau* approach in movies such as *Aguirre: Wrath of God* (1972)[32] and *Heart of Glass* (1976 – in which he also hypnotized the cast! Only in a Herzog production!). It delighted Herzog to simply assemble the cast, have them arranged in *tableau* fashion for the camera, and then – *do nothing* (like Pasolini, Herzog liked to have actors simply standing there).

The intricately detailed interiors in the cinema of Walerian Borowczyk draw heavily on late 19th century decoration and architecture. Borowczyk doesn't do Minimal. Instead, furnishings are rich, colours are deep reds, materials are wood, velvet, dusty glass and embroidered cloth, shelves are crammed with objects, with rooms looking like museums. It's an anal look, of collectors, of connoisseurs, of art lovers.

31 Many of the compositions in *Ordet* are flattened, with the performers arranged in a tight, flat space at right angles to the camera. It's a frontal, *tableau* approach to composition that Carl-Theodor Dreyer favoured in other movies. You might say that action is staged this way in *Ordet* because it derives from a theatrical play, and the film set is a replica of a stage. No. That has nothing to do with it: this is how some filmmakers like to block their actors.

32 *Aguirre* employed stylized *tableaux*, scenes which were consciously staged as paintings or portraits.

One of Walerian Borowczyk's delights are boxes, cabinets, cupboards and display cases of all kinds – but preferrably nice, old wooden ones. The cabinets and boxes often contain mysterious objects, like busts (Borowczyk is fond of statuary of all kinds). The sets of a Borowczyk film are *already* a museum display. They are like a Surrealist exhibition, or the 'secret museum' or 'private collection' of pornography and erotica of the 18th or 19th centuries. Or like a show of curios and antiques, arranged in aged, wooden display cases (recalling the Pitt Rivers Museum in Oxford, England, used so evocatively in Philip Pullman's *His Dark Materials* books).

Who knows where Walerian Borowczyk sourced all of the incredible objects in his films? Clearly some of them are manufactured just for the film, but many are existing pieces – partly because Borowczyk loves objects with a history, objects that have been used. Almost all of the props in Borowczyk's pictures have been used; new, pristine items are very rare in his films. So he must've scoured many flea markets, auctions, antique stores, and art fairs (all the usual places where production designers go. Paris is a good place to find all of that stuff).

The love of wooden boxes recalls all sorts of artists: the Surrealists loved boxes (like Max Ernst), as did the Minimal artists (such as Donald Judd, Carl Andre and Jackie Winsor. Judd, one of the two or three most important artists of the 1960-2000 period, made the box his fundamental form).

But there's one artist above all to consider in relation to the boxes in Walerian Borowczyk's cinema, and that is the reclusive, North American artist Joseph Cornell (1903-73), not least because of the way that Cornell would use his boxes to frame and present an arcane array of objects: a bird, a star map, an egg, a photograph, a feather, a pebble. If you like Borowczyk's films, I'd highly recommend you look at Joseph Cornell's enigmatic art of boxes.

The films of Walerian Borowczyk were low budget productions and they didn't draw on the enormous resources of big, studio movies in the West. Borowczyk and co. were operating in a maverick manner, so they couldn't rely on a vast building containing nothing but costumes (as at Warners in Burbank), or the amazing dock of dioramas (as at Sony/ Columbia in Culver City), or the prop departments of major studios, or their warehouses of furniture.

Aside from *Goto: Island of Love*, Walerian Borowczyk's feature films were made in colour. Some of Borowczyk's animations were in black-and-white. It makes sense that *Goto: Island of Love* should be in black-and-white, but Borowczyk was clearly happy in either medium. (All of the usual constraints of commercial cinema would have operated for Borowczyk – all film producers, distributors and studios argue for colour films, for all the usual reasons – one of the chief ones being – what else? – money. They reckon that audiences don't want to see (or pay for) black-and-white movies, in the age of colour films and colour television). But if you consider the range of techniques that Borowczyk employed in his animation and films, you can see that he was a versatile and adaptable filmmaker. If a producer or studio told him he could only make films in colour or only in b/w or only with three actors or only with one set, he could do it, and flourish.

Walerian Borowczyk was fond of using music that was part of the early music trend, where mediæval and Renaissance music was performed on authentic instruments, in arrangements close to the originals. Thus, much of the music you hear in Borowczyk's cinema is a modern simulation of how music might've sounded in the Renaissance and Middle Ages.

WALERIAN BOROWCZYK'S CLOTHES

Clothes, clothes, clothes, it's all about the clothes in a Walerian Borowczyk film. (You can say the same of the cinema of Vincente Minnelli, Luchino Visconti, Pier Paolo Pasolini and Ken Russell). Even when there is plenty of other stuff going on, Borowczyk's films make time to study clothes. Many historical movies are called 'costume dramas', usually referring to the lovely frocks that the starlets wear. But Borowczyk's films offer a genuine feeling for clothes – how they move on the body, how they hang on the body, how the layers work together, and what is underneath them. Few other filmmakers have filmed clothing like Borowczyk: there is a heightened, sensual apprehension of the materiality of clothes, of textures, colours, shapes, weaves, etc. (Cinema, for Boro, is a means of exploring life, and humans are always inside clothes, always interacting with the world through clothing). Actors get to wear great clothes in a Borowczyk movie.

Walerian Borowczyk could easily have had an alternative career as a fashion designer, or a costume designer for movies. Hugo in *Love Rites* is a fashion designer; there's an *hommage* to designer Mariano Fortuny; Sonia Rykel and Aldo provided costumes for *Three Immoral Women.*

And no other filmmaker has so enjoyed characters putting on or taking off clothes. In *Immoral Tales* alone there are scenes of characters taking off their outfits in every episode, and sometimes it's a slow process, such as when Lucrezia Borgia's father and brother undress her. At times Borowczyk's films look like a costume fitting for a movie. And when characters take off their clothes in a Borowczyk picture, it's usually down to nudity.

Walerian Borowczyk of course loves layers and things that are hidden then revealed, or partially revealed. No one could fail to notice that this filmmaker has a fetish for naked women clad in gauzy, filmy cloth (usually white), white dresses, white wedding dresses, white wraps, white cover-ups, white skirts, white underwear, etc. Nipples and pubic hair are visible underneath; it's a classic look in erotica. To emphasize it, sometimes Borowczyk has actors take off their clothes then put on something see-through.

Corsets are one of Walerian Borowczyk's beloved items in clothing – appearing in films such as *The Beast, Love Rites, Immoral Tales, Jeckyll* and *The Story of Sin* (among others). An actress such as Marina Pierro does look fabulous in a corset. Corsets developed in the 18th and 19th centuries (the forerunner was the bodice of the 15th century); they were typically made from whalebones woven into fabric; a muslin or cotton shift was worn underneath; they were laced up at the front or back (later corsets were made with woven elastic material). Boro isn't alone in reviving the corset (and in dispensing with clothing on top of them) – fashion designers such as Vivienne Westwood took up the corset (Westwood produced push-up corsets in 1987); pop star Madonna helped to popularize them; 1990s designers added short skirts to create evening wear; leather or metallic corsets were worn as vests over dresses; bras were built into business suit jackets (they were made with Lycra or foam).

WALERIAN BOROWCZYK AND RELIGION

Walerian Borowczyk's films are anti-clerical and anti-Catholic; there are many scenes, in movies such as *Behind Convent Walls, Immoral Tales, The Beast* and *Story of Sin*, exploring the moral hypocrisy and sexual repression of Catholicism. At the same time, though, Borowczyk clearly revels in some of the imagery and ritual of Catholicism (like many filmmakers – they can't resist it, having grown up with it),[33] and many of his

33 Japanese animators *adore* Catholic imagery – angels, crosses, stained glass and churches are everywhere in *animé* (but they completely empty it of meaning).

films seem to ambiguously celebrate as well as condemn organized religion (one sees the same ambiguity in the films of Pier Paolo Pasolini, Luis Buñuel and Federico Fellini).

Like Pier Paolo Pasolini, Luis Buñuel and Ken Russell, Walerian Borowczyk delights in exploring the links between sex, death, religion, blasphemy and art. There is the same enjoyment in attacking institutions such as the Church, Catholicism, morality and Christian tenets, using weapons such as Surrealism, humorous irreverence, satire, violence and blasphemy. Oh, and lots of nudity and sex.

Walerian Borowczyk was fascinated by institutions, and often portrayed them – the island stronghold in *Goto*, the convent in *Behind Convent Walls,* the Vatican in *Immoral Tales* and *Three Immoral Women,* and the brothel in *The Rites of Lurve.* And he's also intrigued by dictatorships – Erzsébet Báthory presiding over her house of women in *Immoral Tales*, the Mother Superior in the nunnery in *Behind Convent Walls*, Goto on the island. And Borowczyk was especially adept at depicting the daily life of institutions, and the numerous rituals and daily tasks – the lighting of candles, say, or the preparation of a bathroom for a mistress, or a prostitute preparing for a client, or the decoration of a church. There's a strong impression of the real, daily lives of the people who live in these institutions. It's one of the strengths of *Goto: Island of Love*, for instance: you really believe those people are living in that run-down, shabby place. Borowczyk grounds his fantastical narratives in (illusions of) realism (or, more correctly, his films portray fantasy worlds or secondary worlds in which the rules and the ethics of the worlds are clearly established, and they stick to those rules and ethics, many of which have analogies with the real world).

Sin. The word 'sin' – *péché* in French – pops up everywhere in Walerian Borowczyk's work. Sin (or vice) – and guilt – in the Catholic religion – are right at the forefront of many characters' thoughts. And no one can miss the numerous scenes set in confessionals, as well as churches.

Sin is in St Augustine's definition: 'any thought, word or deed against the law of God'. There are deadly/ mortal sins, capital or cardinal sins, the Seven Deadly Sins, Original Sin, and less grievous sins. Original Sin refers to the first time that humans disobeyed God.

Transgression is perhaps a better term to define a general trend in W. Borowczyk's art – the transgression of social and moral norms, of authorities (and God), of laws/ rules. For narrative forms like cinema, the concept of transgression/ sin is tailor-made – you have a taboo, and then you break it (punishment usually follows). It's a powerful narrative package that you can apply to 1,000s of stories and situations.

The sensual aspects of sin or vice are merely sensationalism (nudity, sex) which act as a hook for marketing and publicity. Rather, it's the breaking of rules, of social/ political/ religious prohibitions, that is the real crux of sin.

Walerian Borowczyk's cinema is full of sins, including vivid representations of the Seven Deadly Sins or Vices – Greed, Pride, Envy, Gluttony, Lust, Anger and Sloth (these appear in pretty much every movie).

Original Sin and the Fall fascinates Walerian Borowczyk's movies – some films are based around them, such as *The Story of Sin* and *Blanche*. The 'Fall' (from what? into what?), once again provides rich material for storytelling. Borowczyk's cinema is full of innocents, pre-Fall characters, as well as *femme fatales*, crooks and worldly-wise characters (Borowczyk's wife, Ligia Branice (b. 1932), always played an innocent Eve before the Fall).

Needless to say, the general trend in Walerian Borowczyk's storytelling was from innocence to corruption, the downward spiral, which leads to the shattering of illusions, the realization that people, society, and the world, are flawed.

HOW TO MAKE A BOROWCZYK FILM

Fancy making a movie in the style of Walerian Borowczyk? You will need the following items:

- candles
- coffins
- mirrors
- slabs of meat
- a horse (and maybe a carriage)
- a harpsichord
- flowers (roses)
- snails (alive)
- quirky, handmade props
- erotic prints
- piles of old books (leather-bound)
- old paintings in fancy frames
- phallic objects
- 19th century/ mediæval costumes
- corsets
- wigs (long hair)
- floaty, gauzy material (white)
- elaborate hats/ headdresses
- a confessional
- a chateau/ old house
- tins of red paint (the default colour for the sets)
- a CD player/ phone/ I-Pod plus giant speakers & amp (for music playback during shooting)
- willing naked bodies (alive)
- and thirty gallons of real pigs' blood

Some of Walerian Borowczyk's other films
(this page and over).

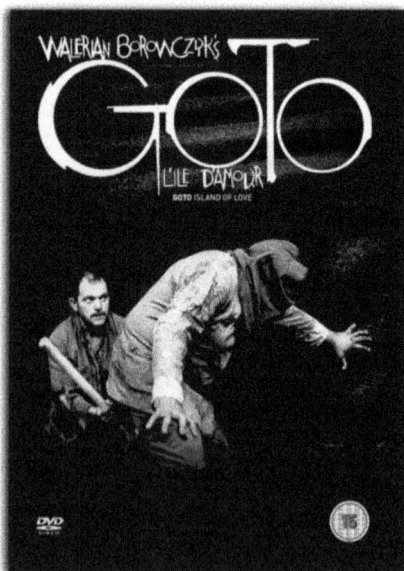

Goto: Island of Love (1969).

The Theatre of Mr and Mrs Kabal (1967)

Blanche (1972).

Three Immoral Women (above).
The Story of Sin (below).

STORIA
DI UN PECCATO

Walerian Borowczyk

La Bête

Jomfruen og
menneskedyret

DVD

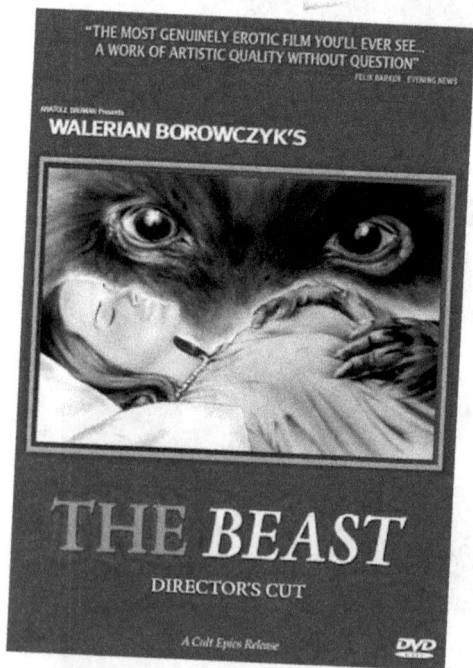

"THE MOST GENUINELY EROTIC FILM YOU'LL EVER SEE...
A WORK OF ARTISTIC QUALITY WITHOUT QUESTION"
FELIX BARKER, EVENING NEWS

ANATOLE DAUMAN Presents
WALERIAN BOROWCZYK'S

THE BEAST

DIRECTOR'S CUT

A Cult Epics Release

DVD

Behind Convent Walls (1977)

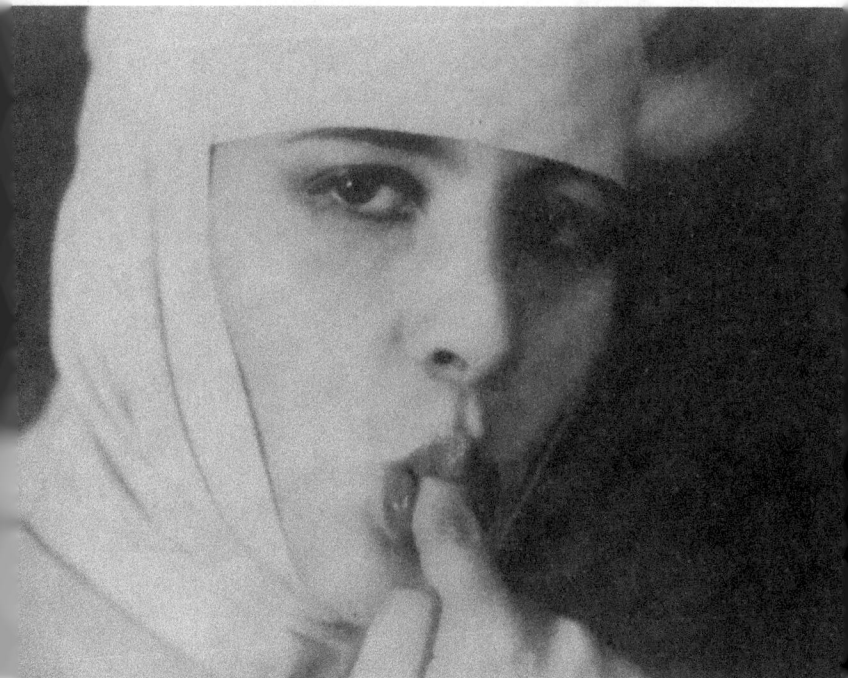

THE ART OF LOVE

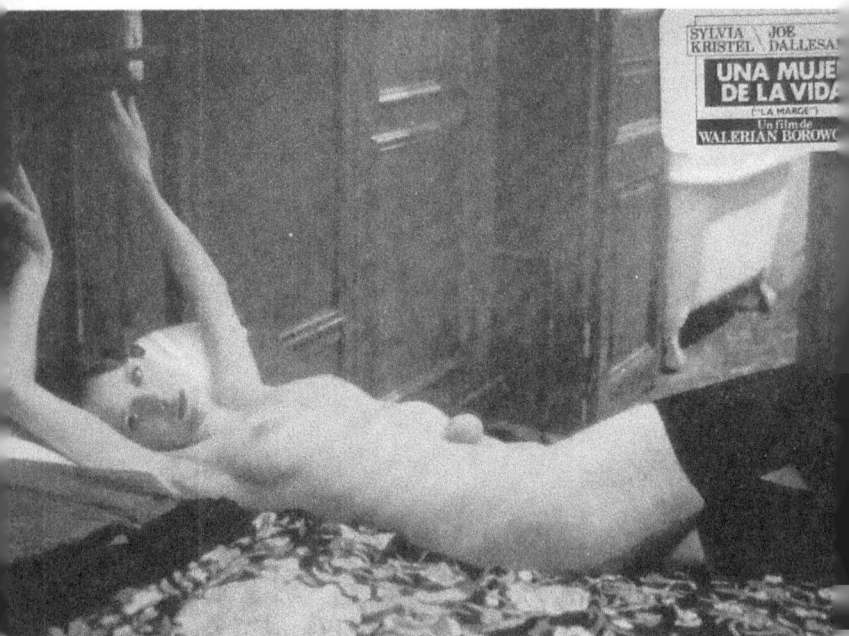

The Art of Love (top). La Marge (below).

The Strange Case of Dr Jeckyll and Miss Osbourne

A Cult Epics Release
LOVE RITES
A FILM BY WALERIAN BOROWCZYK
THE DIRECTOR OF THE BEAST

Two of the last movies directed by Borowczyk: a fine amour fou film, Love Rites, and easily his worst work, Emmanuelle 5.

La mano di Walerian Borowczyk
il corpo di Emmanuelle
Emmanuelle 5
da un'idea di Emmanuelle Arsan

Monique Gabrielle

Dana Burns Westberg

C. Hardester

Yassen Khan

Harold Kay

DVD
VIDEO

DOLBY
DIGITAL

PAL

PART TWO
◆
IMMORAL TALES

I

IMMORAL TALES

CONTES IMMORAUX

INTRO.

Immoral Tales (*Contes Immoraux*, 1974) is a master-piece. Made in French, it was a collection of four erotic stories: *La Marée* (*The Tide*), based on a story by Walerian Borowczyk's friend André Pieyre de Mandi-argues (from *Mascarets*, published by Gallimard); *Thérèse Philosophe*, about a young woman locked up in a room who finds escape in masturbation; *Erzsébet Báthory*, about the original 'Countess Dracula'; and *Lucrezia Borgia*, about the decadent, Italian Renaissance dynasty of the Borgias.

It is, in short, a massive change of direction for Walerian Borowczyk, from *Blanche* to *Immoral Tales*! (Or is it? With hindsight, we can see where Boro was headed!) Altho' many in the production team of *Immoral Tales* were Boro regulars, some of them expressed doubts about what they were filming (reflecting the unease from film critics: should they celebrate a *ciné*-artist who spends so much time on erotica?).

Immoral Tales is also the first of the movies helmed by Walerian Borowczyk that contain a lot of erotic scenes. After *Immoral Tales*, Borowczyk would be associated with arty erotica.

A short film, *Une Collection Particulière* (*A Private Collection*, 1973), a catalogue and documentary of the collection of erotica of both Borowczyk and André Pieyre de Mandiargues, was going to be part of *Immoral Tales*, along with *The Beast* (it was narrated by and starred de Mandiargues). Both *A Private Collection* and *The Beast* were included with the other three tales at some screenings of *Immoral Tales*,[1] until Boro and Anatole Dauman opted to take out *The Beast* (in this cut-down version, entitled *The True Story of the Beast of Gévaudan*), and use it in the feature-length version of *The Beast*, which was released in 1975. (The loose form of *Immoral Tales* allows for the short films to be combined in different ways).

---

1 For example, *Immoral Tales* was screened in London in 1973 and featured *A Private Collection*, *The Tide* and *The Beast of Gévaudan*. *The Beast* was placed third in the L'Age d'Or version of *Immoral Tales* – when it was entitled *The Beast of Gévaudan*.

Contes Immoraux continued Walerian Borowczyk's exploration of the erotic sensibility (for some it was a lapse into pornography, as Borowczyk's next film, *La Bête*, demonstrated for those nay-sayers). It was a time when Boro was working closely with André Pieyre de Mandiargues, a key figure in the production of *Immoral Tales*.

Immoral Tales starred Lise Danvers (an unknown), Fabrice Luchini (an actor who went on to appear in numerous productions; if you watch French cinema regularly, you will see Luchini), Charlotte Alexandra (who appeared in several explicit films soon after this), Pascale Christophe (who was in *Les Héroïnes du Mal*), Paloma Picasso, Florence Bellamy, Boro's friend Mario Ruspoli and his son Fabrizio (under the names Jacopo Berinizi and Lorenzo Berinizi).

Paloma Picasso was the daughter of the painter Pablo Picasso (1881-1973), in her only leading role in a film (aged 25). Born in 1949, Picasso is best-known as a fashion designer (for Tiffany) and for her perfumes. In *Immoral Tales*, Picasso is a calm, restrained presence, which makes her murderous acts all the creepier[2]

Lise Danvers was an unknown actor, and has apparently appeared in only one other film, made around the same time as *Immoral Tales*. Danvers was a substitute for Isabelle Adjani (then starting to make a name for herself); Boro was disappointed that the young Adjani declined. One reason may have been the nudity – Adjani is known for refusing to do nude scenes (such as for Jean-Luc Godard in *Prénom Carmen*, 1983). When Adjani appeared in *La Reine Margot* (1994), for instance, which required sex scenes, she kept most of her clothes on (however, Adjani has done nude scenes elsewhere)[3]

Piet Bolscher was costume designer, Dominique Duvergé was first AD, Bernard Daillencourt, Guy Durban, Noël Véry and Michel Zolat were DPs, and Boro is

2 Observers saw Picasso standing up to Borowczyk, however, and questioning some of his ideas.
3 In *L'Éte Meurtrier* (Jean Becker, 1982), Adjani was 'stark naked for much' of the film, according to David Thomson (I haven't seen *L'Éte Meurtrier*).

credited with production design, editing, and direction. Anne-Marie Sachs also edited. Maurice Le Roux composed the music. *Immoral Tales* wasn't passed by the British Board of Film Classification until 1995 (for the video release).

Immoral Tales was filmed in France and Sweden; the last two episodes were made in Sweden for the financial benefits.[4] *Immoral Tales* won the Prix de L'Age D'Or in 1974 (in Brussels), an award celebrating Surrealism, and the London Festival Choice, when it was shown at the Festival (in late 1973). A memorable outdoors screening took place at Locarno for 2,000 punters: despite a storm, they all stayed to the end (which pleased Boro).

Immoral Tales was apparently second at the box office in 1974 in France among erotic movies. Released Aug 28, 1974. Eastmancolour. *Immoral Tales* is 2,847 metres long. 105 minutes (running times vary – 103 mins and 115 mins uncut).

Immoral Tales was produced by Anatole Dauman and Argos Films, along with Syn-Frank Enterprises. Fellow Pole Dauman (1925-98), one of the key film producers of the period, was an important producer in Boro's career. Dauman had credits that included art house classics such as *Hiroshima Mon Amour, Masculin/ Féminin* and *Mouchette.* Dauman founded Argos Films in 1951, with Philippe Lifchitz. Dauman defined his form of film producing as follows:

> a cinema not of literary adaptations but of cineastes who invent an exceptional relation between the text and the images.[5]

And Dauman defended his films and filmmakers when they ran into trouble with censors. Dauman was the ideal producer for Borowczyk: as director Nagisa Oshima noted:

> having initiated the project in as unambiguous a

4 Dauman also took *Masculine/ Feminine* to Sweden.
5 Dauman in J. Gerber, 13.

manner as possible, he then leaves the author
completely free and trusts everything to him[6]

One of Anatole Dauman's specialities was the
combination of softcore porn and art cinema (or arty
films with plenty of erotic components, taking advantage
of the relaxation of what was deemed acceptable in the
film market in the late 1960s and early 1970s): Dauman
produced Walerian Borowczyk's *Immoral Tales* and *The
Beast*; *In the Realm of the Senses* (Nagisa Oshima),
Fruits of Passion, and *The Tin Drum.* Dauman's *resumé*
on the art cinema circuit (via his company Argos Films)
is impeccable: Alain Resnais (*Hiroshima Mon Amour,
Night and Fog, Last Year At Marienbad, Muriel*), Robert
Bresson (*Au Hasard Balthazar, Mouchette*), Jean Rouch
(*Chronicle of a Summer*), Alexander Astruc (*Crimson
Curtain*), Nagisa Oshima (*In the Realm of the Senses,
Empire of Passion*), Andrei Tarkovsky (*The Sacrifice*),
Volker Schlöndorff (*Circle of Deceit, The Tin Drum*),
Wim Wenders (*Paris, Texas, Wings of Desire*), Chris
Marker (*Sunless, Sunday In Peking*), and Jean-Luc
Godard's *Masculin-Féminin* and *Two or Three Things I
Know About Her.* (At least 8 of those films are regarded
as masterpieces).

Immoral Tales was an anthology film, which were
popular in France and Italy in the 1960s and 1970s –
famous examples include *RoGoPaG* (Pier Paolo Pasolini,
Roberto Rossellini, Jean-Luc Godard and Ugo Gregoretti,
1963), *Loin du Viêtnam* (Alain Resnais, Godard, William
Klein, Joris Ivens, Chris Marker, Agnès Varda and Claude
Lelouch, 1967), and *Amore e Rabbia/ Vangelo '70*
(Bernardo Bertolucci, Godard, Pasolini, Carlo Lizzani,
Marco Bellocchio and Elda Tattoli, 1967).

Anthology films were producer-led projects (like
most movies – and it was true of *Immoral Tales*), in
which a film producer such as Dino de Laurentiis or
Carlo Ponti exploited their contacts and industrial
associations and put together a package of film directors
(typically tackling a common theme, such as modern love

---

6 Oshima in J. Gerber, 140.

and Boccaccio in *Boccaccio '70*, produced by Carlo Ponti and Antonio Cervi). In *Immoral Tales*, all of the segments were helmed by Borowczyk.

Immoral Tales came about when producer Anatole Dauman asked Boro for some short films with an erotic element to put together as an anthology movie. Boro would later contribute to the anthology TV series *Série Rose* in the late Eighties.

So *Immoral Tales* wasn't a pet project that Walerian Borowczyk had been long developing, or a book he had optioned, or a script he had written on spec, etc – it was a project made when a film producer, noting the huge success of erotic movies, asked the director to come up with some erotic stories to put into an anthology piece. It was Dauman who cast actors such as Paloma Picasso and Sirpa Lane.

The music for *Immoral Tales* was by Maurice Le Roux, and also Guillaume de Machaut, Musique Espagnole Ancienne, Musique Hongroise Ancienne, and Walerian Borowczyk's favourite Domenico Scarlatti.[7] In many parts of *Immoral Tales*, the music is exquisite – particularly the recreations of Renaissance and 17th century music (presumably by Musique Espagnole Ancienne and Musique Hongroise Ancienne). The opening credits play with a lovely mediæval piece. The genre dubbed 'early music' in classical music circles is popular nowadays, and Borowczyk makes brilliant use of it. I will keep coming back to Borowczyk's use of music, and how it is overshadowed by the nudity and sex and visual eccentricities of his films.

One of the very striking aspects of *Immoral Tales* is how much of a silent film it is – or, rather, how little dialogue there is. Because it's not silent – there is plenty of music, and sound effects. Long stretches of the film are without dialogue. In the first segment, *The Tide,* André is talking plenty about tides and such, but the sound of *la mer* and the seagulls is just as prominent. In the second film, *Thérèse Philosophe,* most of the

7 Domenico Scarlatti (1685-1757) was part of a musical family, and composed around 600 pieces for harpsichord.

dialogue comes from God, no less, in voiceover. But most of the second film is still without dialogue (tho' many sound effects, as Thérèse uses everything in the room to pleasure herself). In the third movie, *Erzsébet Báthory*, there's a little dialogue from the soldier, but virtually none from the two leads, Erzsébet Báthory[B] and Istvan. The fourth episode, about the Borgias, has much more dialogue – a ranting monologue from Girolamo Savonarola in the pulpit, and the conversations between the Borgias themselves. In this film, though, it's Lucrezia Borgia's laugh, teasing and scornful, as much as the dialogue, that stays in the mind.

Immoral Tales travelled back in time: the first story, *La Marée* (*The Tide*), was set in the present day, the following stories moved back to the late 19th century (1890), to 1610 for 'Countess Dracula', and finally to Renaissance times with the Borgias (to 1498). The first episode was set in France; judging by the chalky, white cliffs in *The Tide*, and clues in the dialogue, it was somewhere in Northern France. The second film was also set in rural France. The third film, about 'Countess Dracula', moved to Eastern Europe; and the final movie to late fifteenth century Italy.

The general opinion from critics and fans seems to be that *Erzsébet Báthory* is the most dramatically satisfying of the four tales, and the most 'cinematic', and that the first two – *The Tide* and *Thérèse Philosophe* – are the weakest. On some viewings of *Immoral Tales*, I find the *Borgias* episode a little disappointing after the boundless invention of *Erzsébet Báthory*, which, possessing such a strong, dramatic impact, makes the flaws of anything that follows show up. *Lucrezia Borgia* is thematically, politically and socially outrageous, but it does not pack the cinematic punch of the *Erzsébet Báthory* episode. (A better order for the episodes might be putting the *Borgias* earlier, and closing with *Báthory*. In most anthology movies, you put your weakest segments

8 Partly, in Báthory's case, to make her more mysterious and unknowable (in the usual way of villains in cinema). And maybe words and language are not possible in a realm of sacrificing young women.

in the middle – same with a live concert, or an evening TV schedule, where weak shows are sandwiched between strong shows.[9] But of course, with home entertainment formats, viewers can watch them in any order. Indeed, *Immoral Tales* was screened with different segments).

The opening titles and title cards of *Immoral Tales* are in a white font over black – i.e., the type of credits employed by prestige filmmakers (Pasolini, Bergman, Allen, etc). The credits are accompanied by period instruments music (as if we're still in the world of *Blanche*, Boro's previous movie as director).

Immoral Tales opens with several quotes – each story has its own literary quote or written intro, on a caption card[10] (including Francois de La Rochefoucauld). It's how to flatter your audience: a French erotic movie that's set in France and playing to a French audience can't go wrong by quoting La Rochefoucauld).

---

9 It's called 'hammocking'.
10 In a Renaissance-style font.

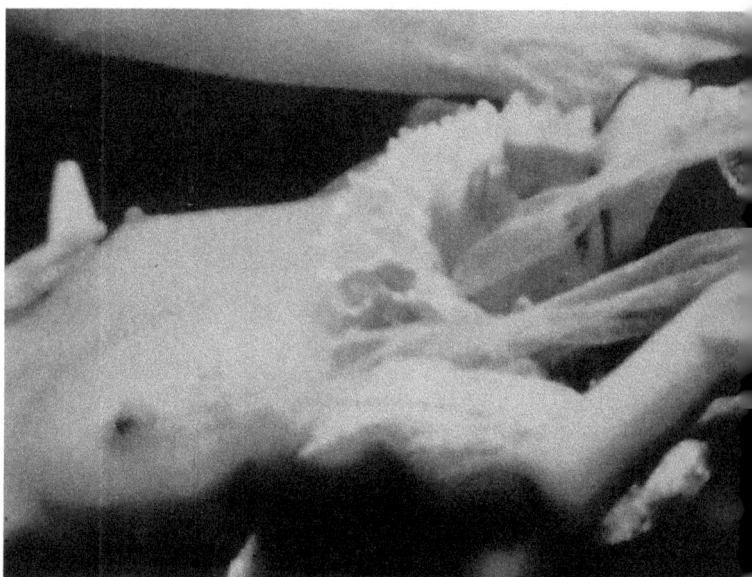

Pablo Picasso's daughter Paloma as 'Countess Dracula' in Immoral Tale

One of Walerian Borowczyk's
favourite subjects in art,
Leda and the Swan, which
The Beast replays.
Here are versions by
Leonardo da Vinci, top,
Veronese, top right.
Peter Rubens, left,
Giovanni Boldini, bottom left,
and Luciano Castelli, below.

Asked who'd he like to be in
history if he had the choice,
Borowczyk said: 'if I have to
choose an epoch and an identity,
it would be that of Leda's swan
in antiquity (if she really was as
beautiful as the artists
represent her)'.

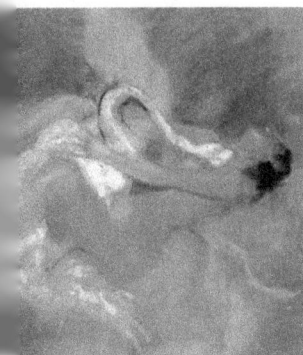

LA MARÉE (THE TIDE)

A title card of a quote from Francois de La Rochefoucauld's (1613-80) *Maxims* appeared after the opening titles. The first story in *Immoral Tales* was about 25 minutes long,[1] and featured two cousins, a 20 year-old youth André[2] (Fabrice Luchini) and a 16 year-old girl Julie (Lise Danvers) cycling to the beach, climbing along some rocks under the cliffs and making love. So far so familiar, but this is not a piece of softcore porn. There's never been a sex scene on the beach like this in cinema (or pornography); this is *very* far from the porn circuit of the San Fernando Valley, or the Euro-erotic cottage industries of Paris or Roma.

The Tide is a very typical movie of its time that combines arty filmmaking with eroticism. It ticks so many boxes:

• It's filmed in French, made in France, with French actors and characters.

• The *milieu* is bourgeois France (check out that big house!).

• It has intellectual/ poetic pretensions.

• It's filmed in a self-consciously artful manner.

• It alludes to painting.

• It features female nudity, and the woman servicing the man.

• It depicts a vaguely sadomasochistic relationship (with hints of a ritual).

• The editing is in a mosaic or collage form.

• And it contains many Borowczykian touches (it fetishizes clothing, for example).

The Tide is simply plotted: a scene at a country house... a bicycle journey along lanes... clambering across rocks on a beach... the couple on the beach... the orgasm... (structurally, it's a cereal packet plot).

There is a scene of the youths at a large, rural house, setting the locale in contemporary France (with some

---

1 You get *The Tide* as part of *The Beast* on DVD; *Immoral Tales* is also now available on DVD and Blu-ray.
2 André takes his name from André Pieyre de Mandiargues, author of the story.

pedestrian exposition, partly from André): Julie waves at some parental figure who departs in a Citroen (with the parents out of the way, the children can play; Julie and André prepare to cycle off to the beach). The landscape they cycle through seems to be Northern France – it might be Normandy, or Brittany (Julie mentions Couville, a small town inland of Cherbourg). The imagery is of Summer, a day out, innocence[3] (only the way that André is ordering Julie about[4] and seems to be planning something hints at other things going on). It's another of several sadomasochistic relationships in Boro's cinema (tho' this one is milder than some of the others). However, this excursion seems to be André's idea (and, along strict gender lines, it's the girl who prepares the food, while the boy fixes the bikes).[5] There are hints, too, in the close-ups that the film selects – in particular, Julie's mouth,[6] which becomes the central motif of this chapter of *Immoral Tales* (along with the sea).

In *The Tide*, there's plenty of play between notions of speaking and showing, between language and the image. Or as the film has it: André *speaks*, but the film *looks* at Julie and her body. Men speak, but women simply *are*. (Certainly André is leading the sequence dramatically, with Fabrice Luchini partly performing the role as a slightly bossy, older brother figure).

It's significant, perhaps, that Julie and André are cousins, or maybe it's just another of those standard tropes in erotic fiction that mask incest (a connoisseur of erotica like André Pieyre de Mandiargues would surely know all about brother-sister incest in the history of pornography, and cousins is a way of evoking it). It's certainly significant that André is 20 and Julie is 16 (and a virgin). He tells her that in Paris each Wednesday he

3 The film selects close-ups of the bikes, including the inevitable fetishist's shot of Julie's ass on the saddle. What did actress Lise Danvers think when this was being filmed? There's a bunch of guys in a car behind me filming my butt!
4 André is a bit like a film director: there are hats (always with the hats in Boro's *œuvre*!), and André says no, not that hat. So Julie dutifully takes it back inside.
5 She bites on a tomato – which foreshadows the penis, and makes a change from Eve's apple.
6 The first of the extreme close-ups in *The Tide*.

visits prostitutes with his friends (oh, right – doesn't every kid in modern literature brag about that?). André seems to be visiting his cousin from the city (the house appears to belong to Julie's folks).

Before any sex can occur, the filmmakers have the couple spending quite a while clambering over seaweed-strewn rocks and trudging along a stony beach at low tide, in and out of the surf. Throughout this, the film builds up images of the beach, the cliffs above, birds flying into their nests, and gulls soaring above the waves. It's permanently overcast (well, it is in many of the shots). More exposition is slipped into some of the dialogue (André, a sexual predator in blue sun hat and wellies, asks Julie about the five boys she's seen, and if they kissed her on the mouth. Yes, the mouth again in Monsieur Boro's work).

André persuades his cousin Julie that they won't get cut off from the tide: he carries a newspaper clipping with the tide times on it, which he places on a rock, beside his watch. The girl seems to be complying mutely and passively to what the youngster wants (the boy is leading the narrative all the way; he talks about educating his cousin). Julie, arriving at the destination after André, goes for a swim in the milky, grey sea, against his wishes (André is literally working to a timetable).

The boy asks the girl to take off her black bikini and leave her see-through, white cotton dress on (a key Borowczykian fetish, found throughout his work). He then asks her to blow him while he explains to her about the tides. When the tide reaches its height, at 11.27, he explains, he will come and flood her mouth, and she will understand about the sun, the moon and the tide. It'll be a gift from the sea, he tells her. (This is the intellectual, French way of seducing a girl, instead of the usual corny lines, it's flimsy, pseudo-philosophical poesie about the cosmos.)

The prelude to the sex act in *The Tide* has Julie undressing, and the camera lingering on her breasts and vulva in a tight close-up, in the familiar voyeuristic gaze of mainstream and pornographic cinema (the woman's body is on display at many points, while André barely undresses – just pulls his jeans down a little but keeps his wellington boots on, a typical Borowczkian touch – and there's a shot of their legs entwining).

So far, so normal: well, kind of. Up to this point, though, the film has constructed painterly images, of the cliffs, the rocks, the waves, birds on the cliffs, gulls floating on the water, the pebbles, and the people dwarfed below the cliffs (in a slow, Kubrickian zoom shot that tilts down from the cliffs to the beach). The imagery evokes the French Impressionist painters and 19th century landscapists who created canvases similar in content to this (Boudin, Sisley, Pissaro, Monet, Renoir, etc).

The editing in *The Tide* is in a mosaic, poetic style (Anne-Marie Sachs and Boro edited). Along with landscape painting, the cutting recalls Cubism, the fragmented, multiple views of an object or an event. The editing pattern breaks with continuity editing many times.

The editing of *Immoral Tales* also includes parts of shots that no professional film editor would show their producer or director. No cutter on the lot at Warners or M.G.M. in the Golden Age of Hollywood would dare to show producers David Selznick or Jack Warner shots like these as part of a completed fine cut (like an out-of-focus shot or a two-second-long blur when the camera operator was adjusting the framing).

Julie undressing and the camera lingering on her naked body is thus just one element among many elements, because Walerian Borowczyk's camera also dwells at length on the cliffs, the beach, the rocks and the sea. No porn director would waste precious 35mm film stock on such images. But Borowczyk seems just as interested in the setting, in the sound and sight of the surging swell, as in the couple making out. (The birds are simply another form of life, like the humans below – and people making love is no different from nature doing its thing).

André and Julie embrace; to prefigure the blowjob, there's an extreme, abstract close-up of the girl's mouth, with the boy's finger stroking her lips, circling round and round, then pressing inside it. It's a classic device to show what isn't allowed to be shown in softcore cinema (the 'meat shot' of sucking), but the filmmakers have the shot go on much, much longer than a conventional art film or softcore flick. *The Tide* returns to the close-up of the girl's mouth a few times; after the sex act, the film again concentrates on Julie's *bouche*, her fingers absent-mindedly pressing her wet lips.

Immoral Tales features luscious close-ups of the girl's face staring up into the camera, as Julie looks at André and listens to him as he explains what they're going to do. It's another game, but a special game, André says, in which she'll learn something about the tides and the sea. (Walerian Borowczyk has a magical ability to film women in close-up, staring into the camera – not every filmmaker can do it – the same radiant, soul-revealing shots appear in *Behind Convent Walls*, of Ligia Branice, for instance, and of Marina Pierro in *Love Rites*. The shots evoke Anna Karina in *Pierrot Le Fou* (1965), which were in turn inspired by Harriet Andersson in *Summer With Monika* (1952), both movies of doomed romances by the sea).

The couple move from the rocks to lie on the banks of stones at the high tideline. André uncovers Julie's breasts and plays with her nipple. When she's working on him, he pulls up her white dress, to reveal her ass and vulva – and the camera lingers over such details, framing nothing but Julie's genitals.

The filmmakers render the everyday world, the surroundings (the stones, beach, rocks, cliffs, sky and sea) strange by cutting away from Julie with her head between André's legs to the waves, the seagulls flying above the spray or the nests in the cliffs (the film cuts, for instance, from that lengthy close-up of Julie's kiester to an abstract shot of seagulls whirling in the sky). The roar and hiss of the ocean builds, until it is very loud, giving the scene a powerful rhythm (the scene plays without music, like many sex scenes in Walerian Borow-czyk's cinema). In Production Code-era, Classical Holly-wood films, cutting away to a shot of pounding waves was a clichéd trope for what couldn't be shown, people making whoopie. Here, in *Contes Immoraux,* it's as if the boy and the girl conjure up the elemental powers of nature, of the sea and the sky, by their lovemaking. The roaring waves illustrate (embody) the couple's sexual energy, in the tried and tested metaphorical manner of poetry (poets have used these tropes for at least 3,000 years), but it also works back in the other direction: the raging sea seems to be infusing the lovers with a primæval erotic power. The *mise-en-scène* is primitive, archaic, with only André's watch, the clothes and the tide timetable as relics of the modern age (though set in the 1970s, the scene has a timeless, mythical quality).

Then, an extraordinary cut occurs, a long shot of the couple writhing on the beach taken from a boat not far out to sea, approaching the shore. In a medium shot, taken from a reverse angle, above the couple on the stones, with the waves behind them, André climaxes, thrusting his hips upwards, his legs entangled with the girl's; the high tide washes over them from time to time, drenching them (the actors must've hated shooting it – *very* cold water, hard stones, no wet suits – aside from that flimsy bit of cloth, poor Lise Danvers is naked – and you can bet that Monsieur Le Auteur asked for more than one take!).

It's like the famous scene in *From Here To Eternity* (Fred Zinnemann, 1953) between Deborah Kerr and Burt Lancaster – well, actually, it's way beyond that scene. *Immoral Tales* has taken up the cliché of sex-on-the-beach, which *From Here To Eternity* and other movies have drawn on, and given it a European, art film spin. The waves pounding the beach and drenching the couple don't need any gloss: *The Tide* has made manifest what other films hint at then draw back from showing.

It's a genuinely erotic sequence – and that's not entirely because of the sex act, or Lise Danvers' nude body, or Fabrice Luchini's quirky personality. It's partly to do with the pictorial and aural elements that the filmmakers have orchestrated here. And it's also to do with the setting – being by the sea *is* erotic, and you don't need actors in films to reveal that to you (artists have been doing it for millennia).

La Marée evokes notions of time, tides, rituals, bodies, skin and sexual fluids, as well as presenting an erotic act. What's memorable about the piece is not the sex, which has been seen a zillion times before, but the interconnection between the bodies and the landscape; the ritualistic aspect (these are not individuals or personalities having sex, but archetypes); and the way the filmmakers manage to turn the ordinary into the strange (or to reveal the strangeness in the ordinary – a profound and absolutely essential function of art). It must rank as the weirdest blowjob scene in all cinema.

The elements of *The Tide* are deceptively simple: a boy, a girl, and a beach. It's the way Walerian Borowczyk and the team orchestrate these apparently plain ingredients that marks the director out as a master. And it's the way that Borowczyk and co. *balance* and *mix* those elements. A Borowczyk movie is never *one thing alone*, never *just* arty, or *just* porny, or *just* comical, or *just* surreal, or *just* bitter. You could send a thousand film students to the coast armed with a camera, tripod, microphone, lights, a couple of actors, food and 2,000 feet of 35mm film stock, and none of them would come back with something as impressive as *La Marée*. [7]

❖

What is *The Tide* about? Many readings suggest themselves. [1] Feminism. A second wave feminist reading might explore exploitation, sadomasochism, patriarchal power, etc. Taken literally, or straight, *The Tide* is pure masculinist fantasy tarted up with some philosophical blether (from the man, of course) about time and tides. The (sexual) objectification of women, the control of female agency with patriarchal language, the woman servicing the man, it's all there in *The Tide*.

7 DP Noël Véry revealed that part of *The Tide* had been filmed indoors, because the weather had been so bad. The studio shots are mixed with the location seamlessly.

But *The Tide* is open to any reading, like any artwork (like anything). For example, it's a *movie*, not an essay published in *Pompous Criticism Monthly*. It's a cinematic work, not wholly reducible to words or themes or issues. What a movie *is* or what it *does* is *not* just about the story, the characters, the themes and other concepts and categories borrowed from literature and theatre.

[2] Painting. The short film evokes elements that have little to do with the psychological manipulation of one human being by another – the lyrical evocations of the natural world, for example. The film suggests a continuity between the natural world and the human world (which can be interpreted in many additional ways).

[3] Magic and shamanism. The fusion between the natural and the human realms evokes magical and shamanic layers in *The Tide*, linking it to Surrealist art (and to the Hermetic, occult maxim of 'as above, so below', or, in modernist terms, the continuity between inside and outside).[8]

---

[8] The youth poetically fuses what the couple are doing with nature with his layer of adolescent lyricism (timing orgasms with the top of the high tide, for example).

A nice day at the beach in The TIde

I'll forget you, so it'll be more exciting
when we meet at the beach.

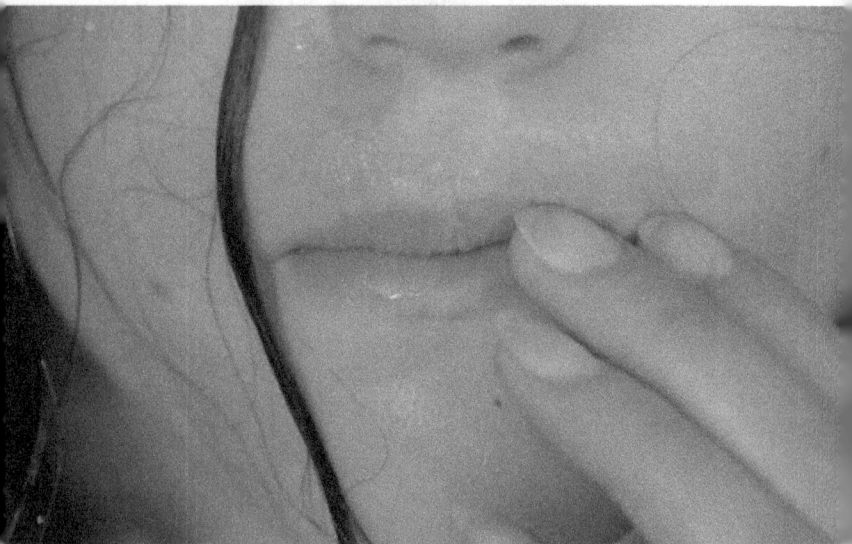
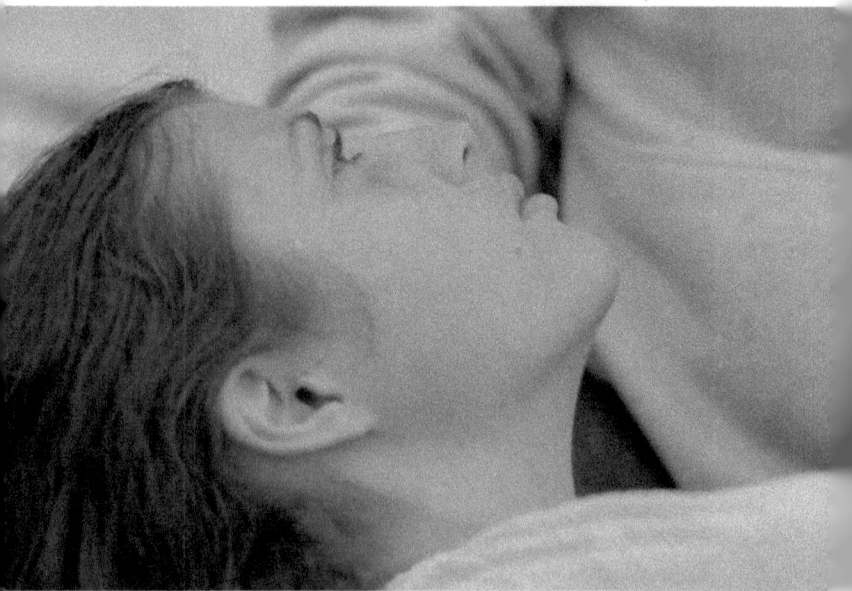

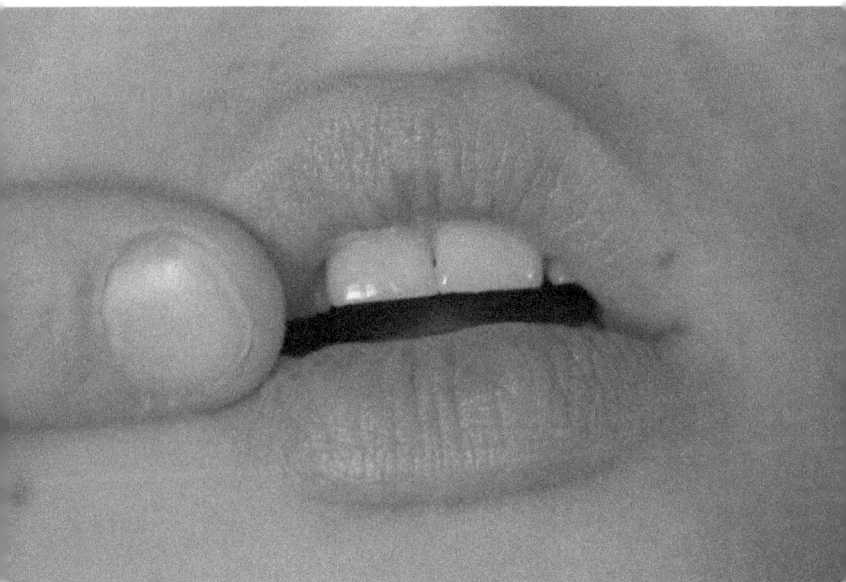

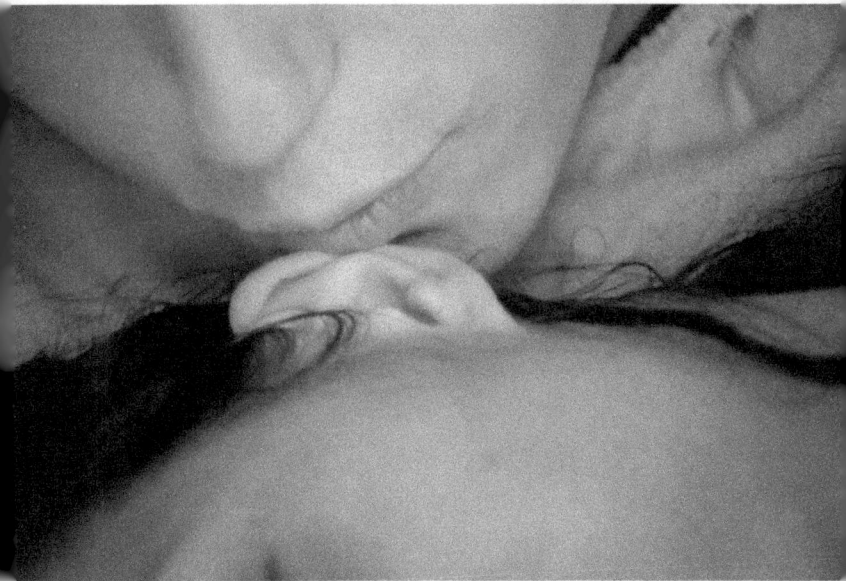

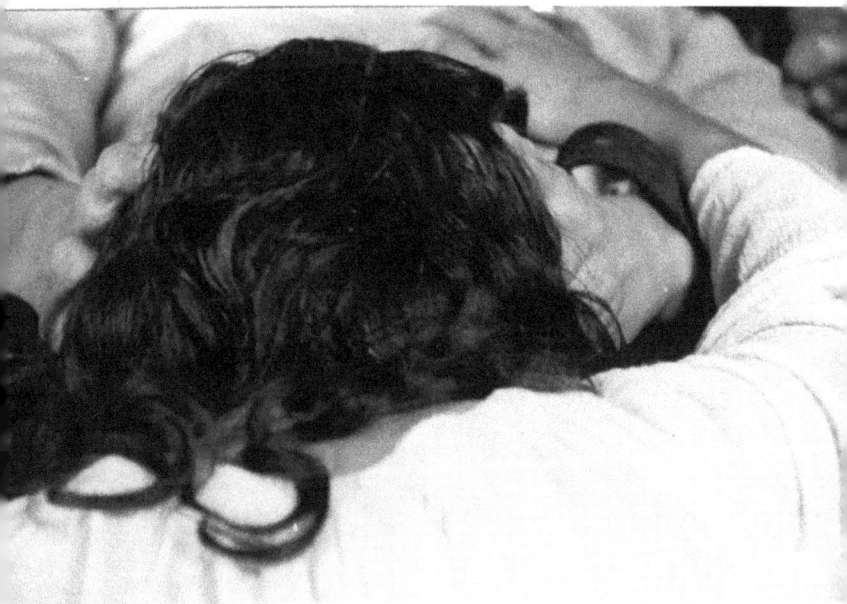
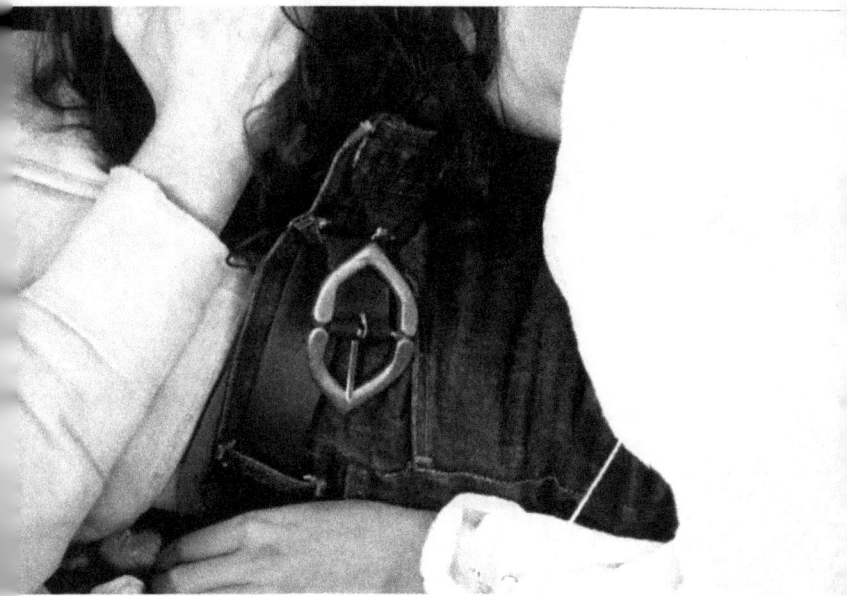

THÉRÈSE PHILOSOPHE

In the second segment of *Contes Immoraux* (around 23 minutes long, and filmed with 16mm reversal stock),[1] *Thérèse Philosophe*, a world of Victorian repression and culture is evoked: a young woman, Thérèse (Charlotte Alexandra), is locked in a room for three days by a stern matriarch. Thérèse is young, naïve, curious, attractive, pale, and clad in a virginal white dress. It's set in July, 1890. It was based on (or inspired by) an 18th century novel (1748) by Jean-Baptiste de Boyer, Marquis d'Argens. The novel was used more as an allusion, rather than an adaptation, and the episode only took up the idea of Thérèse being locked in a room for two weeks, surrounded by erotica, but trying to refrain from masturbation.

British actress Charlotte Alexandra (b. Nov 19, 1954) was found by Boro's assistant director Dominique Duvergé when she was working at the Elite model agency. It was one of the 20 year-old Alexandra's first films (she had one previous credit),[2] but she soon went on to several productions with sexual content, including *A Real Young Girl* (*Une vraie jeune fille*, 1976),[3] *L'Acrobate* (1976), and *Goodbye Emmanuelle* (1977), in which Alexandra was depicted in many sexual scenarios. Alexandra also did nude magazine photos. (Later, Alexandra worked in British television, and in movies such as *Personal Services*, 1987).

It's not an easy role: Charlotte Alexandra has to appear fully nude and in big close-ups for much of the piece. Many actresses would not even consider such a challenging and revealing role. And it's not only nudity – it's full-on sex. And it's Alexandra appearing alone in most of the episode – she has to carry the whole thing.

The sequence in *Immoral Tales* consists of a

1 Which gives *Thérèse Philosophe* a different look from the other episodes in *Immoral Tales*. It looks like Kodachrome film stock, with distinctive red and warm hues (while the skin tones of actress Charlotte Alexandra seem a little bleached out).
2 *Les Baiseuses*, a.k.a. *Jailbait* and *That Girl Is a Tramp* (1974).
3 Directed by one of the most over-rated directors in the modern era, Catherine Breillat.

woman's masturbatory fantasies – at the beginning of the segment, Thérèse visits a church. (A shy, demure girl in a church, what could possibly go wrong? In the cinema of Borowczyk, plenty!). Thérèse is filmed in a richly decorated, Catholic church (apparently after Mass), suggestively caressing brass columns, eagles, statuary and church organ pipes, in the Ken Russell, jokey-phallic manner[4] (accompanied by Walerian Borowczyk's beloved classical organ music). This was reprised with the nuns in *Behind Convent Walls*.

Here, a deep, male voice (identified as the voice of God,[5] no less) prompts our Thérèse to reveal herself to Him sensually, to live for Him as she should. A second voice, a young woman's, seems to be questioning God (but politely and submissively, of course); this may be Thérèse voicing her inner doubts.

The church scene introduces W. Borowczyk's recurring themes of spirituality and sexuality, God and love (and how Thérèse interprets God's request for love erotically: God may ask for love (like he needs it! what half-decent deity could be bothered with the love of mere humans?), but humans will interpret that command differently).

The opening scene of *Thérèse Philosophe* is steeped in Catholic imagery and religious repression – a young woman wandering around a church in an erotic daze and fondling statues and long, metal organ pipes provocatively is fairly blatant and to the point. Walerian Borowczyk doesn't hold back (in this area of narration, he seldom does!): this young woman is sexually curious, the film says.

One of Walerian Borowczyk's cinema's recurring scenes is a young person (usually a woman) learning about sex acts for the first time. She's inquisitive, wants to know more, wants to do what she's heard about (or, more often in Boro Land, seen in antique erotic books). So films such as *Immoral Tales*, *Three Immoral Women* and *The Beast* depict young people having sex for the

---

4 Churches were never built to be used like this!
5 It sounds like André de Mandiargues.

first time (often it's masturbation). (The first time is endlessly fascinating to artists and writers, of course – not only the 'first time' in sex, but with any experience. That Borowczyk keeps returning to the portrayal of virgins is, from the viewpoint of conservative society (and feminism), another black mark against him. It's partly a dramatic choice, how drama automatically intensifies a state or a relationship).

An authority figure is mandatory here, setting the boundaries, the laws, the social context, etc (thematically, psychologically, dramatically) – this time, it's a mother/ guardian figure who chases Thérèse around the garden (a rather silly scene – because she was late coming home from church, or because she did ungodly things at God's bidding). Once the mother figure's done her duty (hurling the girl roughly into a lumber room), she, like the parental figure in the previous episode, *The Tide*, disappears.

Thérèse has a *Station of the Cross* (*De la Croix*) which she hangs onto (she hysterically begs her mother/ guardian for it repeatedly when she's locked in the room. Yes, a girl's going to be OK if she's got her copy of *The Stations of the Cross*! Today it's a cel phone – don't leave me alone for *three days* without my cel phone! I'll die of boredom! – but in them days, a little religious book could save your life).

The stern matriarch grudgingly gives Thérèse her beloved *Stations of the Cross* tome, and then chucks in her hat and... some cucumbers. Oh man, of all the 1,001 items of food Old Mother Goose could've thrown into the room for Thérèse, it had to be *cucumbers*! In a Walerian Borowczyk film![6]

Girls and cucumbers...

It's a joke, right? Or the pay-off to a joke: *'and then she [-----] with a cucumber'*. Surely Borowczyk, the arty, intellectual filmmaker, is not going to do *that*?

Oh yes he is!

(And the geeks, critics and intellectuals look on in horror from the wings as their revered Superstar Surreal-

6 In a Ken Russell film it's bananas!

ist Abstract Artist descends to the sleazy depths of filming girls being naughty with cucumbers...).

Locked in the room, Thérèse finds objects for her erotic fantasies: a book of 18th century pornography, called *Thérèse Philosophe* (Borowczyk's love of erotica, and cataloguing it, manifests itself in the sequence where the young woman leafs through the book at length, and the film cuts to close-ups of the 18th century, black-and-white illustrations of people tupping in a variety of settings and positions).[7] So the episode partly comprises a montage of erotica, a mini-documentary about Ye Olde Eroticke Bookse, with the audience looking at someone looking at erotica (as in *A Private Collection* and *The Beast*).

The sex act inevitably dominates all of the other aspects of *Thérèse Philosophe* in film criticism – but the episode is not entirely about female sexual *jouissance*. For instance, there are several beats where our Thérèse, bless her, is doing nowt more extraordinary than trying on accessories and seeing how they look on her in the mirror (some glasses, a hair comb, etc).

Boro sometimes complained that viewers saw the sex and ignored everything else that was happening in his works: here in *Thérèse Philosophe*, we see a teenager indulging in simple narcissism, in dressing up, in smiling at herself when she finds something that works.

As well as the book of erotica, *Thérèse Philosophe* also cuts to paintings in the room, and many other objects (the editing is again in Boro's familiar allusive/poetic montage): Walerian Borowczyk and the team have art directed the set with a host of antique items: a bust; a mirror; a chamber pot; several old trunks; a shelf of leatherbound books; embroidered pictures; a white bed spread; corsets; a large, wooden doll; erotic photographs and postcards; and a fairground wheel.[8] It seems to be a lumber room, maybe a former nursery. A world of the

7 Some of these are by artists illustrating Jean-Baptiste de Boyer, Marquis d'Argens.
8 There might be a conveyor belt, off-screen, with assistants picking up the knicknacks and handing them to the crew, who place them in the scene.

past, with hidden mysteries, like the erotic photos Thérèse finds at the bottom of the trunk (after taking out many clothes). Like other Borowczyk heroines, Thérèse embarks upon searching through the room for things to use, discovering the cache of French, 19th century erotica in a suitcase.⁹ Maybe they were her father's (which adds the familiar father complex element to the depiction of female sexual curiosity).

Thérèse's erotic desire knows no bounds. As in Walerian Borowczyk's other films, once women have become sexually aroused and intent on orgasm, nothing will stop them. By the end of the second episode of *Immoral Tales*, everything in the room has been appropriated by Thérèse for her masturbation session: a print of Edward VII (!),¹⁰ a bath mat, a large, wooden doll, the flowers on her hat, candlesticks and cucumbers. She takes up the battered, wooden doll and kisses it on the mouth softly. Memories of childhood.

There's no music in *Thérèse Philosophe*, except in a couple of bursts: strident organ music is deployed when Thérèse discovers the book of erotica: it's as if she's discovering sex (i.e., life) for the first time. Oh, so *that's* what adults get up to she maybe thinks (it's sex, but it's also new life, new experiences – a new world). The 1974 film cuts back from the erotic prints to a C.U. of Thérèse reacting to them, disturbed and aroused, with over-cooked, silent movie acting.¹¹ The burst of religious organ music is sort of awkward and stupid, too, like something out of D.H. Lawrence's fiction (when Lorenzo turned all preachy and pompous, and, *oh!, lo and behold,* Connie Chatterley trembles with another super-dazzling rush of pleasure).

It's one of Walerian Borowczyk's main themes: a young person discovering new vistas or experiences. That it's eroticism or self-pleasure is merely a sensational

9 Probably from Borowczyk's own collection, including a selection of saucy postcards which T. contemplates.
10 That's one of Borowczyk's themes – the all-consuming erotic power of women. Candles and cucumbers might be expected to be part of masturbation, but not a print of Edward VII (England's ugliest king) or a bath mat!
11 She puts her fingers to her mouth in her anxiety.

hook for a piece about awakening (after all, the film producer, Anatole Dauman, asked for erotic tales). But it could be about many other secret or unknown areas of life.

God's voice talks to Thérèse. It's Joan of Arc time, voices of God in the head time – except God didn't tell Joan of Arc to masturbate with a cucumber! (which is how our heroine interprets what the Lord commands). Thérèse undresses and offers herself to the deity, lying back on the bed, clad in a favourite Walerian Borowczyk costume, a white, cotton dress. Her heart is open: she is ready. She starts to masturbate, first caressing her nipples, pulling off her dress, then squeezing her thighs together. The camera lingers longingly (and for a *long* time) over Thérèse's pale skin and pink nipples. Flash-backs occur – to the church, as if Thérèse is riffling through some erotic moments in her life, to find some images she can use for her masturbatory fantasies.

Thérèse takes up a cucumber and traps it between her thighs. Again, the camera lingers over the girl's body as she pleasures itself, abstracting her body in multiple close-ups. Finally, Thérèse sits up, her back to the camera, and pushes the cucumber inside herself, gradually working her arm faster until she is ramming it in, and gasping loudly, accompanied by the squelchy sounds of the cucumber in her Holy of Holies.

I guess some viewers would see this scene as pure soft porn. Porn as Art. Art as Porn. Whatever. But the filmmakers are doing other things within the scene, such as cutting away to the objects that are included in the girl's masturbatory trance: the paintings of aristocrats on the wall, the Edward VII lithograph, the wooden doll. Towards the end, Thérèse gropes for her *Stations of the Cross* book, where she keeps a portrait of a man (possibly someone she admires); as she kisses the portrait, it's the final trigger for her orgasm.

✳

Much of the *Thérèse Philosophe* episode in *Immoral Tales* is shot in painterly close-ups of the woman's body, panning from her mouth to her breasts, or along her torso to her heiny, which abstract (and fragment) the sexual act into a series of beautiful images. The camera travels over the woman's writhing body in big close-ups, refusing to clarify exactly what's going on, and emphasizing the erotic significance of details. (Pornography, by contrast, uses medium shots to include the whole body, and close-ups for clarification. And mainstream, Hollywood cinema tends to use these same big close-ups as Borowczyk, but not for abstract, painterly reasons: rather, in order to avoid showing the whole, nude body, for censorship reasons, to deliver a particular kind of product to a particular audience, yet with some of the same aims as pornography).

As Thérèse reaches her orgasm, she sits on the bed with her back to the camera, thighs spread apart, and the shots consist of close-up expanses of pale skin, accompanied by Thérèse's frantic moans. Only after she comes does the camera pull back to clarify the situation, and show Thérèse moving, to lie face-down on the bed.

The allusions to paintings do not stop there, though: Thérèse lying face-down on the bed recalls 17th and 18th century nudes and odalisques (and in particular François Boucher's famous painting *Mademoiselle O'Murphy* (1751), which Borowczyk would know. Even Hollywood movies have referenced the famous Boucher butt).12

Walerian Borowczyk's penchant for frontal, flattened compositions is apparent throughout the scene: the bed is set against the wall, and the camera stays back, flattening out the elements within the frame. Where most film directors might have blocked the action in flattering, three-quarter views, covered in medium shots (and with pretty back-lighting) – particularly if they had prima donna movie stars who insisted on looking great – Borowczyk favours a cinematic approach all his own. At the end of the scene, for example, Thérèse lies on the bed,

12 Louise O'Murphy, the model for François Boucher's famous nude *Mademoiselle O'Murphy*, became King Louis XV's personal prostitute (his 'mistress', as critics call them), after the King saw Boucher's painting. The high art 'possession' or pleasure of the female nude in Boucher's painting became the real 'possession' of Louise O'Murphy's body. Clearly, kings can 'buy' what they like: they can have the best art, and 'have' the best women.

but the composition is end-on, looking down from her head (perhaps evoking the art of Christ entombed after the Crucifixion).

✳

A coda ends the episode which takes *Thérèse Philosophe* into another area of historical erotica: the young woman pounced upon by a lecherous, older man in a field (as the caption at the top of this episode explained). First, Thérèse escapes from the room into the sunny fields (including a very lengthy shot as she disappears into the distance, a composition that recalls 18th century landscape painting. Right at the end of the scene, a stocky, middle-aged, grey-haired guy appears, and poor Thérèse cries for help. A rape is suggested, but not shown, because the second episode ends abruptly, right there.

It seems as if Thérèse is going to be punished after all for her masturbation and erotic feelings. It seems that God didn't intend her to show Him her love by loving herself with a cucumber. (The coda is silly and insubstantial, and the film isn't interested in it at all: it's ineptly filmed; it looks as if the film crew lavished all of six minutes on it before breaking for lunch; it comprises only two or three shots (most of it is the long shot of the field), and some images of cows looking indifferent; and it has the appearance of a scene demanded by financers or producers, to balance/ round off what's gone on before).

Thérèse Philosophe's coda is one of those scenes that are deliberately thrown away, dismissed with an impatient flick of the wrist by the filmmakers. *They* are not interested in it (therefore *we* aren't, either). This 'can't-be-bothered' attitude occurs in the cinema of Borowczyk occasionally.

✳

Some viewers found *Thérèse Philosophe* the weakest segment of four naughty tales in *Immoral Tales*. It seemed rather pointless for some, while others found it the most erotic segment of the lot. Certainly, it's so eccentric and idiosyncratic, only one person on Earth would've made it. It is pure Borowczyk.

Let's not forget that it was a striking and brave performance by Charlotte Alexandra, too: she gives herself wholly to the piece. No matter what the filmmakers might be doing, no matter what fancy stuff the film crew might cook up, much of the impact of *Thérèse Philosophe* derives from Alexandra's acting. Film directors can direct, and writers can write, but it's the *actors* who have to embody their ideas on the screen.

The scenario was potent enough for Walerian B. to return to it several times: women masturbating on their own pops up in *Three Immoral Women* (the follow-up to *Immoral Tales*), in *The Beast*, in *The Art of Love*, and in *Behind Convent Walls*, among others.

THEORIZING *THÉRÈSE PHILOSOPHE*

So, what is *Thérèse Philosophe* 'about'? Is it –

• The story of a young girl who masturbates in a room?

• The sexual initiation/ maturation of a young woman in late 19th century Europe?

• An excuse for more female nudity?

• A Guide to Art Direction for the budding production designer? (Tip: visit every flea market, thrift store, junk shop and auction room and buy everything you can made between 1860 and 1920).

• How to make a film with a girl, a cucumber, and some saucy postcards?

• A pretext (i.e., excuse) for another visit to (or recreation of) an Erotic Museum?

• How young, white women in Europe said *Shove It* to repressive social regimes in 1890?

• How girls conduct self-therapy on the troubled relationship between mothers and daughters?

• A hymn to sexual self-healing?

• A 'take back the night', pro-feminist rant (using the politics of mid-1970s feminism)? (We could explore the film in terms of 1970s French feminism, such as the writings of Luce Irigaray and Hélène Cixous about female *jouissance* and how it challenges patriarchy and the Law of the Father).

• Masturbation as performance art[13] and political protest? (Masturbation as revolution).

• The self-assertion of individuality? Or the individual within the social system?

• A pæan to the power of the imagination to alter life? (Outer as well as inner life)?

• A savage attack on Christianity? On organized religion?

• An ironic deconstruction of political/ ideological/ religious issues such as hypocrisy, oppression and totalitarianism?

---

13 Several performance artists in the 1960s and 1970s used masturbation as part of their art. Mike Kelly masturbated (while naked, of course) with cuddly toys, and Vito Acconci hid under wooden ramps in art galleries and masturbated while speaking to visitors.

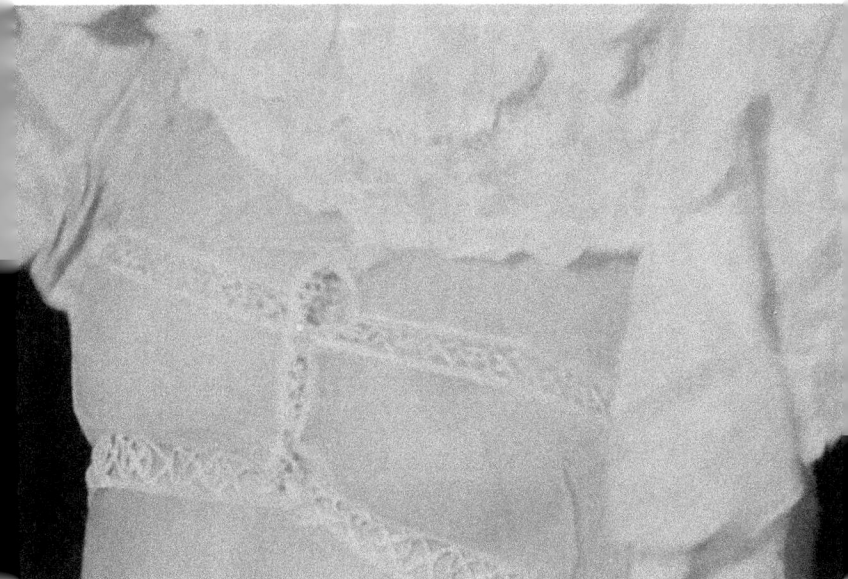

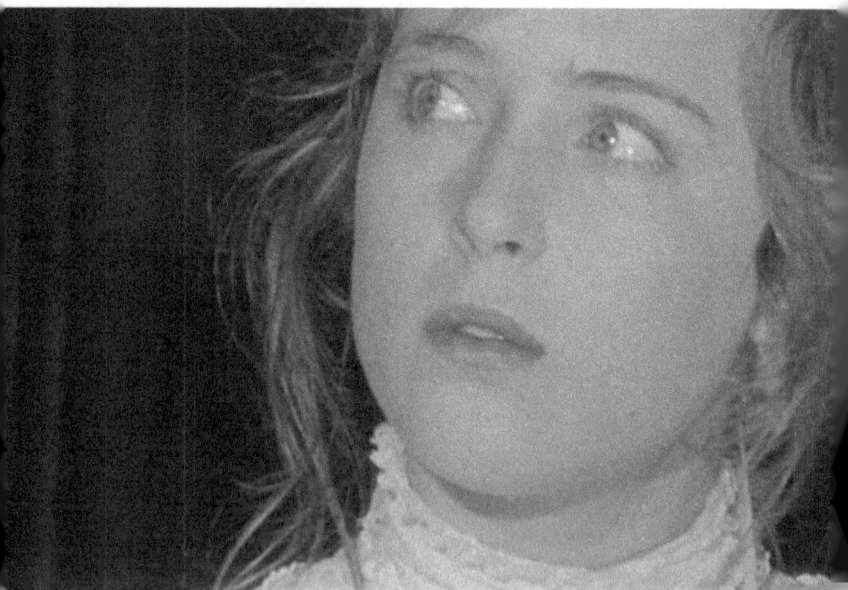

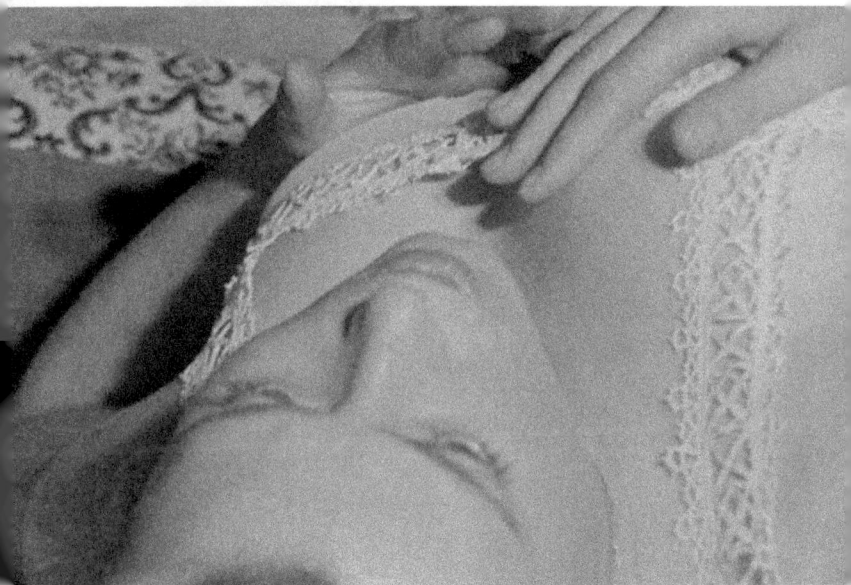
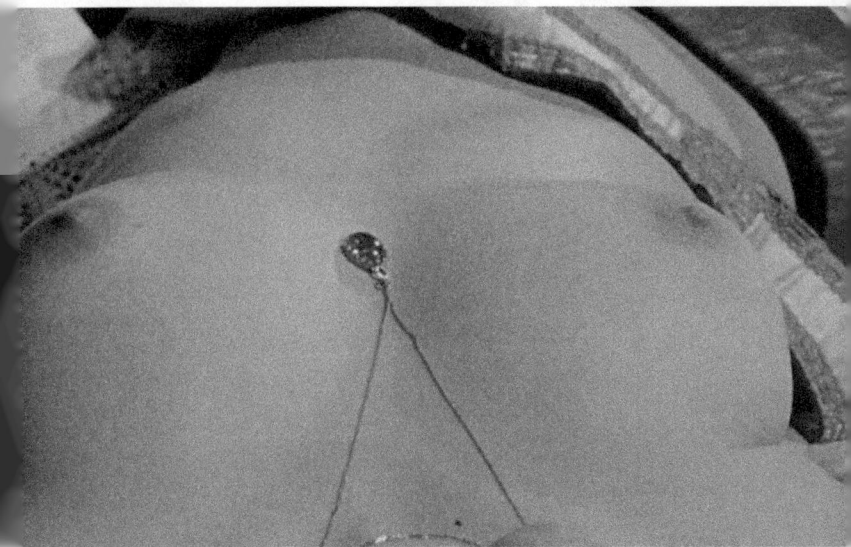

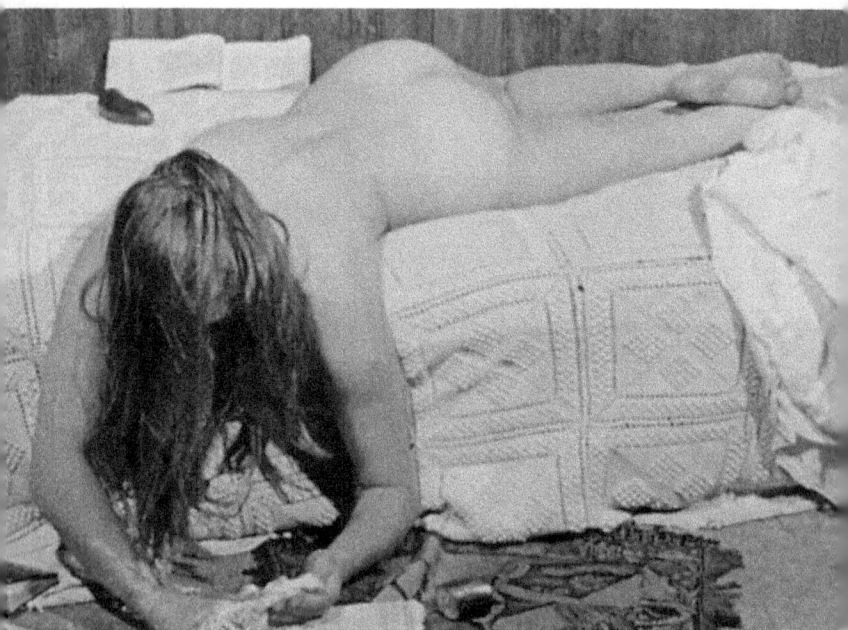

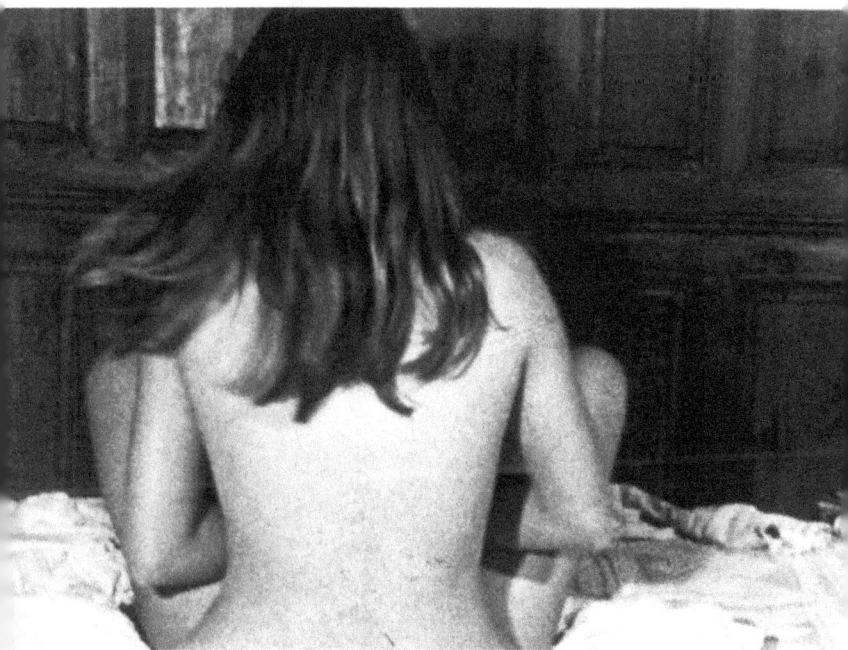
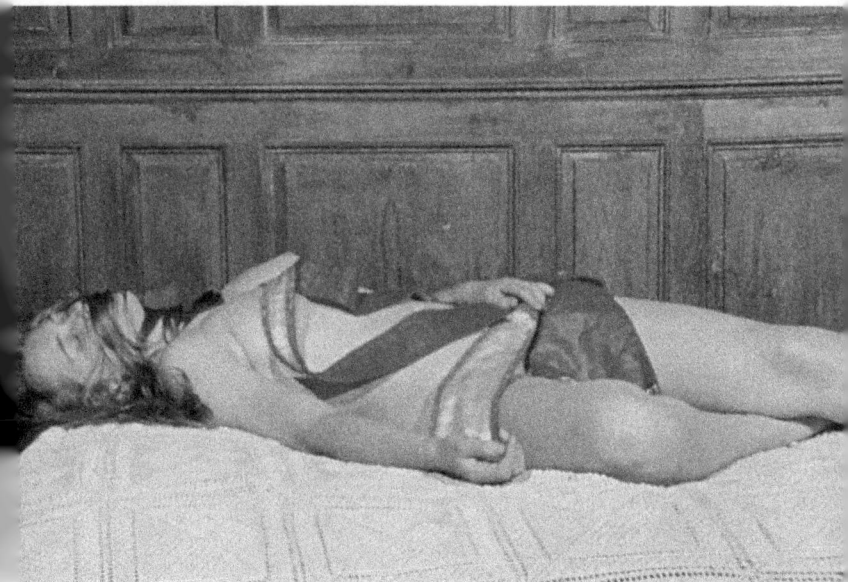

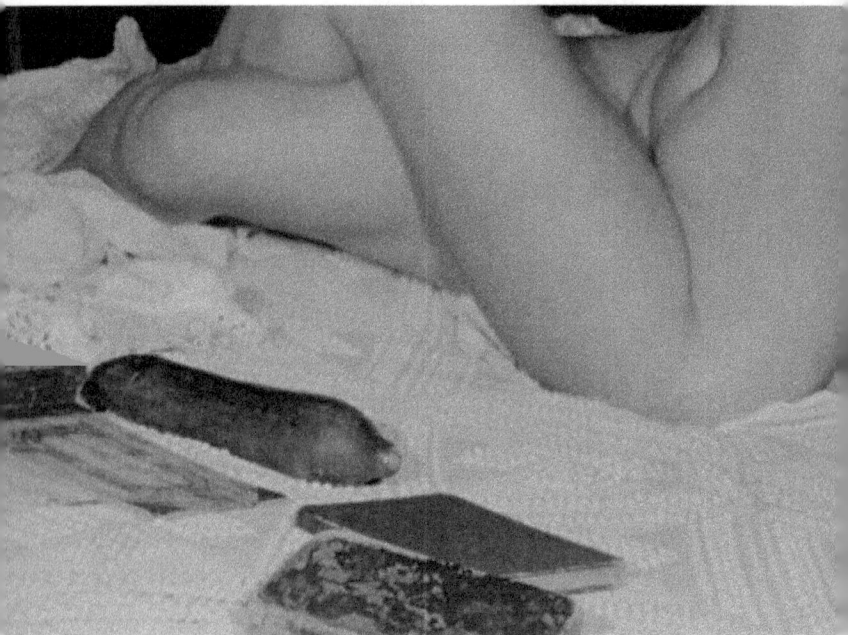

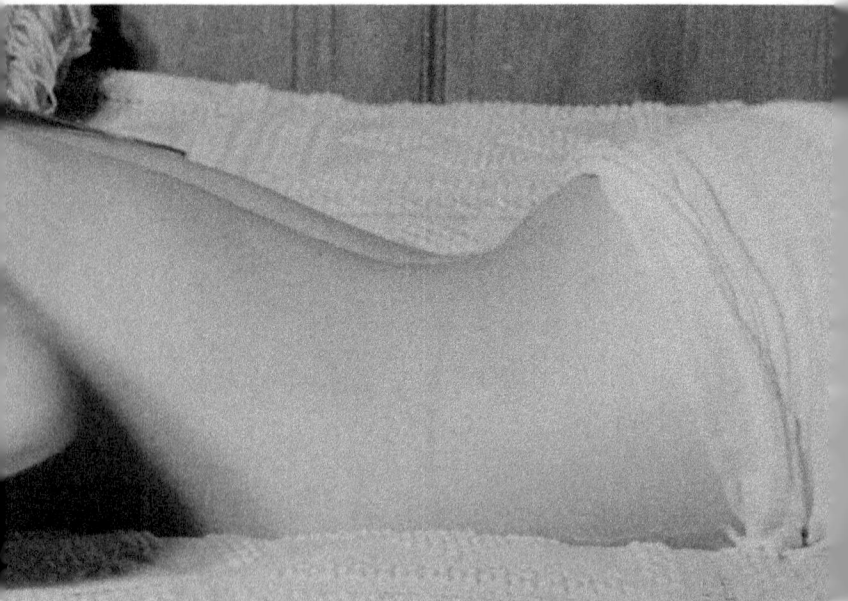

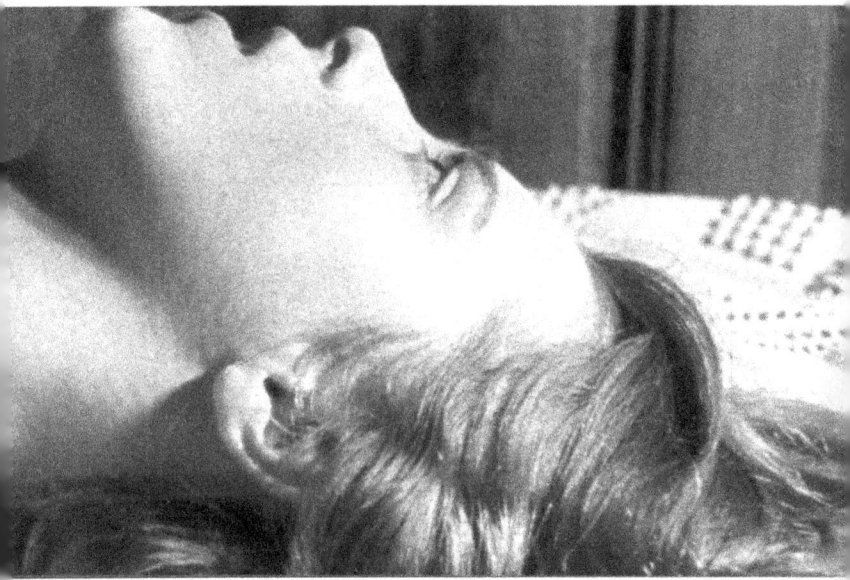

The third episode in *Contes Immoraux*, *Erzsébet Báthory*, is one of Walerian Borowczyk's finest outings in cinema. It works so well partly because it starts from a very strong concept, has a solid script, and is delivered with a truly inspired cinematic genius. This is Boro working at full power.

Erzsébet Báthory is set in 1610 in Eastern Europe, and opens with the Countess Báthory (Paloma Picasso) riding on a black horse accompanied by her aide Istvan (Pascale Christophe) and some soldiers. The setting is Hungary (tho' filmed in Sweden). This episode drew on *The Bloody Countess* by the Surrealist poet Valentine Penrose (1898-1978), wife of British Surrealist Roland Penrose.[1]

There's a brief evocation of the Dracula myth, a little cinematic, Gothic atmosphere: a roadside crucifix which the Countess glowers at, and birds cawing ominously in the sky. Most of *Erzsébet Báthory* plays without dialogue (in giant close-ups of eyes reminiscent of Christopher Lee's Dracula; eyes are often the focus of attention in vampire stories – to the point where, in recent vampire movies like the *Twilight Saga* or the *Underworld* series, contact lenses are deemed mandatory).

The music in *Erzsébet Báthory* is wonderful early music (which has to be the most pleasant and refined music ever put to scenes of mass murder. The music is fantastically mismatched with the scenes of grotesque carnage; the music is so light and airy, it might be the background sounds for a gardening show on television (today we're visiting Versailles, folks – watch out for the hands lunging out of the graves).

The real Erzsbét Báthory (1560-1614) was known as 'the Blood Countess' and 'the Bloody Lady of Cachtice'. She lived at Cachtice Castle and is one of the most notorious serial killers in history: she was accused of 80 deaths, but some witnesses said 600 or 650. (And she was a very nasty piece of work, with legend attributing to her

1 The book's still available.

all kinds of horrors and tortures, not only murder). She had men and women as lovers (including from the peasant class). She was very rich, and well-connected.

Countess Báthory was one of a number of historical figures in the early modern period who became infamous for their bizarre, blood-filled exploits: Vlad Dracul, the Wallachian prince in the late 15th century (supposed ancestor of Dracula), and the alchemist Gilles de Rais (1400-40) who murdered 200-300 children in the pursuit of the philosopher's stone (Borowczyk wanted to make a feature about de Rais).

Immoral Tales isn't the only movie about Countess Báthory: there have been European flicks made in the 1970s, as well as films featuring female vampires (sometimes with lesbian elements) – around 30 films about Báthory in all (including *Countess Dracula* (1971) and *Daughters of Darkness* (1971)). The 2008 movie (*Báthory*) starring Anna Friel and *The Countess* (2009) are among the latest.

There are novels, etc, too. *Carmilla* (1872) by Sheridan Le Fanu was often an inspiration (Bram Stoker was apparently inspired by *Carmilla*). The first Italian vampire movie, and the first, proper, Italian horror movie (C. Tohill, 20), *I Vampiri* (*The Devil's Commandment*, Riccardo Freda, 1956), was a version of the Countess Dracula legend.

Hammer, the British film studio, produced *Countess Dracula* in 1971 (although it stars horror diva Ingrid Pitt, it's not a patch on *Immoral Tales*. *Countess Dracula* is one of those flicks you think halfway through: *why am I bothering to watch this?*).

❋

In *Immoral Tales*, Countess Báthory is clad (in the first outfit of several costume changes), in an enormous, black feather hat, and a lush, black costume, complete with an enormous, black cloak, in the tradition of movie Draculas (it's a self-consciously over-the-top costume). Istvan, her cross-dressing aide (dressed as a page), wears white in silk (and rides a white horse; Báthory's mount is black of course).

The costumes are *fabulous*. Those hats! And boots! And cloaks! And corselets! Piet Bolscher,[2] Borowczyk's regular costume designer (including the costumes in *Immoral Tales*), should be mentioned here (and the make-up and hair artists). *Immoral Tales* is truly a costume drama. It's a proper *costume* drama. It's all about the clothes (and characters are undressing and dressing frequently, too). This director knows how to film a costume.

The costume design of *Erzsébet Báthory* draws on the great Italian designers such as Danilo Donati (Pier Paolo Pasolini and Federico Fellini), Piero Tosi (Luchino Visconti and Fellini), and Piero Gherardi[3] (Fellini); one imagines that Paloma Picasso, a fashion diva herself, contributed ideas. (Paloma Picasso has been heavily involved with the French fashion industry for many years – a world where being over-the-top is expected, darling.)

The *Erzsébet Báthory* episode next cuts to a village scene in rural Hungary, where the calm of people going about their everyday business is interrupted when the Countess's soldiers invade the pastoral scene[4] and offer to take away the young women of the village (primarily set in a farmyard, we see old women gossiping, a woman treading veg (?) in a barrel, others cutting them up; but the first vignette of a typical day in the countryside of Hungary is a stereotypical, 19th century illustration of pastoral erotica: a young couple making out in a barn spied on by a young girl). The village scene has the appearance of a woodprint of the era of Pieter Brueghel

2 Piet Bolscher worked mainly on productions directed by Borowczyk.
3 Piero Gherardi not only designed the costumes, he was also production designer and art director, and a key contributor to the cinema of Federico Fellini. Formerly an architect (and a real Count), Gherardi is responsible for a significant proportion of the visual splendour of Fellini's works. Gherardi and Fellini met in the mid-Fifties, and got on famously (they first worked together on *Cabiria*). As Fellini put it, Gherardi grasped what he was trying to do immediately: 'Even before a film has taken complete form in my head, he has understood what it's about about, the atmosphere, and comes up with ideas and sketches which clarify things for me'.
4 As soon as a bell is sounded, everyone scurries indoors.

or Albrecht Altdörfer, or a Dutch painting of the 17th century of everyday life.[5] (The producer Anatole Dauman's daughter, Florence, was part of this scene.)[6]

When some of the women resist, and try to escape, the guards turn violent. The scene turns into an attack, with soldiers pursing the women all over the place (including a scene where the woman tupping in the barn is chased through a stream in a field, with her partially-dressed boyfriend leaping on the soldier to defend her. In the not-very-convincing scuffle, the soldier seems to strangle the guy).

The filmmakers include all manner of details in this sequence, including the classic images of an abandoned baby crying, an old man hiding, and people struggling to escape. It's clear that the soldiers are only after young women (the voyeur girl and the baby are also examined by the visiting aristos, but the movie doesn't depict them as part of the group of victims taken to Castle Báthory. That would be too much, perhaps – children and babies on top of 25 young women. That the baby is brought out for the Countess to examine is an example of Boro's black humour).

After rounding up suitable candidates, Countess Erzsébet Báthory appears on horseback (circling the victims intimidatingly). The soldiers line up the women to be inspected. After examining the women (pulling up their clothes to reveal repeated close-ups of breasts and crotches), they are taken to the Countess's home. The scene sexualizes and cruelly objectifies the victims – it's quite different from the usual scene in movies where some lord inspects a potential slave's teeth, as in *Spartacus* (1960). It's clear from the outset that the Countess is interested in the women sexually; she wants fresh women (not necessarily virgins, although virgins

5 The rural activities come from late Summer, even tho' it's visibly Mid-Winter, and the puddles are frozen over. The extras must've been absolutely freezing, because Piet Bolscher has put them in only two layers, or one layer for some of them (partly to make the examination scene easier to film).

6 She recalls that when Dauman saw or heard about the proposal of nude scenes, he was furious. (So, no nude scenes for Florence).

are part of this kind of crude, blood and guts myth). Here, the Borowczykian fetishized close-ups of part of the (usually female) body take on a very creepy tone (after all, *Erzsébet Báthory* is filmed from the perpetrators' point-of-view).

At the Báthory mansion,[7] the naked body count of *Contes Immoraux* increases dramatically (as opposed to Hollywood's *dead body* count), with seemingly endless shots of naked women in showers, washing each other, giggling, talking, walking down corridors covering their breasts, kneeling and praying[8] in front of a Christian shrine (a wooden crucifix),[9] as good girls should, and, eventually, being ushered into a large, red room by the ever-efficient aide, the Countess's inner sanctum (the 'bloody chamber' of fairy tales).

The elaborate preparation of a glass of wine[10] (red, of course) when the story switches to Báthory's digs evokes the Mass, inevitably, and the blood that the Countess will bathe in (Báthory hands round the wine to the naked victims in a ritualistic gesture). There are also many other shots of minor details in this set art-directed to perfection, such as a painting[11] of one of the Countess's ancestors holding a sword (or maybe it's the Countess herself, in the manner of these tales, whose life's been artificially lengthened).

This film set is a classic, Borowczykian environment: it's the ultimate seduction setting: a large room with wooden panelling and deep red walls (dark green below), dominated by an ancient, carved, wooden bed. It has been meticulously lit by DP Bernard Daillencourt. (Unlike some of Borowczyk's sets, this was constructed in a

---

7 We only see the interior.
8 Alas, their prayers come to nothing, and this particular god doesn't materialize in beams of light to save them from the Countess.
9 A deliberately ugly Christ, it might be a prop from an Ingmar Bergman movie like *The Seventh Seal* (this episode was filmed in Sweden, after all).
10 The swivelling cupboard for the wine and the ornate glasses is a classic bit of Borowczykian production design.
11 They are filmed handheld, as if we're right up against them.

studio – partly, probably, because so many naked extras[12] were required, and logistically and economically a studio's a better idea (and for the comfort of the participants). The episode was filmed in Sweden for financial and logistic reasons).

The set also evokes, without it being stated, that the Countess has been doing this for a *long* time: notice that there are several showers and changing rooms leading off the corridor (complete with peeping tom mirrors angled above them or on the opposite walls). That is, the castle has been adapted for the bathing, processing and mass extermination of women – exactly like a concentration camp. (Istvan even ticks off what seems to be the victims' names, adding an air of officialdom to the proceedings – which, as they all die, seems pointless. But the old habits of bureaucracy persist)[13] Boro had explored the issue of the death camps in *Angels' Games* (1965).

As in other Borowczyk films, the bathing scenes in *Erzsébet Báthory* evoke the 19th century painting tradition, where bathing was a justification for showing women nude (in the art of Leighton, Alma-Tadema, Moreau, and Ingres). The way that the naked extras are lovingly photographed (in even, diffuse light) recalls those artists (and the early tradition in Renaissance art of portraying Goddesses bathing, often with a male figure spying on them, like the Goddess Diana with Actaeon).

Most of the first half of the *Erzsébet Báthory* sequence concentrates on showing the group of nude women in the showers and bathrooms, the camera lovingly panning over their naked bodies, again and again (the film returns to the showers several times, becoming an extended riff on the bathing scene in *Goto*). The movie concentrates time after time on women soaping their breasts, asses and vulvas (some of the montages are two minutes long). Some of the women wash each other. Bernard Daillencourt's camera lingers

12 The extras were hired in Sweden, where Boro was hoping for the blonde, pale-skinned women of Scandinavia (and was apparently disappointed when not all of them were).
13 The text is in Boro's distinctive handwriting.

unashamedly over close-ups of vulvas and nipples. It's a paradise of female nudity.

It all seems to be a grand build-up for some extra-ordinary erotic encounter. There are no men in this scene: apart from the group of some twenty-five naked women, and the aloof, aristocratic Countess herself, there is only her aide Istvan, another woman, dressed as a page (tho' presumably the victims see Istvan as male, wielding a phallic sword). This 3rd part of *Immoral Tales*, *Erzsébet Báthory*, seems to be in part both an eroticist's fantasy of lesbian sex and group sex, and some bizarre ritual which can't be reduced to mere titillation or porn.

Walerian Borowczyk & co. have created the ultimate seraglio, a boudoir, a convent full of young, naked women. Borowczyk is clearly in his element here: in one scene he has the women coming down the corridor, exploring it, then kneeling in front of Christ on the Cross, and praying (in a single scene you've got nudity/ women/ coercion/ exploitation/ submission/ Christianity/ relig-ion). Istvan also crosses him/ herself before the sacred icon).

Istvan and Báthory both spy on the women as they bathe, using tilted mirrors mounted above the showers (Walerian Borowczyk's art direction is inspired; this is voyeurism taken to mass-mechanical, industrial levels). Meanwhile, the row of showers automatically has sinister connotations: this is not a bunch of innocuous cubicles at a swimming pool or a gym. Even if the viewer doesn't know the story, we've already seen women being taken under coercion. (It turns the proceedings even more sinister by having the actors play the scenes exploring the castle like children, rather than women in their late teens or early twenties. As if, once you've been selected as a victim, you start acting like a victim).

The 1974 film plays with different gazes: the Count-ess is presumably lesbian or bisexual (or seems to prefer women, as portrayed here), but Istvan is at first depicted as a young man, who appears to be enjoying the abundance of women. Only later, during a lesbian clinch with the Countess, is Istvan revealed to be a woman. But after Báthory has been arrested, Istvan embraces and kisses the captain of the soldiers. So she starts off as a heterosexual boy, shifts to a female lesbian, then a heterosexual woman (one wonders how she got the job of Báthory's aide in the first place. It was probably a helluva interview). Notice how quietly methodical Istvan is, suggesting that s/he and the rest of the Countess's underlings have been doing this for a long time.

Some of the women draw graffiti on the walls in charcoal – images of penises, of course (one woman draws an oval with lines sprouting out of it and says it's the sun, but it's the standard graffiti vulva). One of the bonuses of *Immoral Tales* is watching Pablo Picasso's daughter going around the showers and rubbing off the pictures of peckers – especially in view of Picasso's late erotic work, the series of mythological prints, where impotent Tiresiases watch people tup (Walerian Borow-czyk would have known Picasso's work). Even mass murderers like to keep their showers clean. The irony and hypocrisy is incredibly bitter.

From the group nude prayer scene (only in a Walerian Borowczyk film will you see a cluster of naked women praying to a statue of Jesus), the movie moves closer to the bloody chamber of fairy tales. First the victims gather around the main doors, climbing on chairs in order to see the preparations on the other side. Again, with the cast of lovely, young actors ranged on a table and chairs, with their backs to the camera, the film indulges in some more close-ups of their butts, thighs and legs.

The regression of the women to children continues with a brief vignette where two women make off with some of the Countess's loot, and are caught by Istvan (they are roped together and led away by the page).

The over-abundant amount of objectified, female flesh enhances the horror with every shot. The victims are not individualized, or named, or even given dialogue: they are kept as one mass of humankind. Their victim-hood is paramount – they have already become fodder for Countess Báthory. As soon as Báthory lays those big, brown eyes on them, back in the farmyard, they are victimized.

The naked women are led into the chamber of horrors by Istvan. Throughout the episode, Walerian Borowczyk and assistant director Dominique Duivergé have asked the extras to be animated, natural, excited. In the bedroom, the excitement gets louder, as the women explore the room in clusters, touching the carved bed, and the furnishings. (The performances continue the infantilization of the victims; when people are reduced to children, they are all the easier to manipulate and torture).

When the Countess herself enters, you know this is the climax of the sequence – partly because the film has reached the big set, partly because Báthory is in amongst the naked virgins, and partly because you know something extraordinary is going to happen. Maybe a mass game of Scrabble? Maybe the Countess is going to be serviced by the women one by one? But she is 'Draculina', so we know she's going to dispatch the women. How is she going to do that?

But *Immoral Tales* does not show the mass murder. Instead, it heads off in a much more interesting direction. It's unexpected that when the Countess enters the scene, the women gather tightly around her as she moves among them, first admiring her clothes (a gauzy, revealing version of the white dress). But then the naked women jostle her, and converge on the carved bed, where Báthory has ended up, and start to rip the Countess's clothes apart, as if stealing the shreds as some token or religious relic. A movie star and her groupies... a queen and her subjects... a demon and her victims.

The scene in *Erzsébet Báthory* becomes a series of medium close-ups of writhing limbs, skin and hair as the women become more violent and hysterical (the editing pattern makes the cuts shorter). They steal the Countess's jewels, some of them eating them (there is a shot of a woman inserting a pearl between her labia, a typically

Borowczykian image).[14] Báthory has her clothes ripped off her in tatters, and the women fight over the pieces. The tearing sounds are loud on the soundtrack, as well as the screams. The scene reaches a crescendo of violence as the naked women scratch each other, drawing blood.

It's a scene with a primal basis, going back to the mænads and bacchanalian or Dionysian rituals of Ancient Greece. And it's an extraordinary addition by the filmmakers to what seemed to be the Dracula myth:[15] a mass seduction which would run smoothly towards death for the women. Maybe there would be glimpses of some infernal machine out of Gothic, mediæval horror through a doorway, and the women would be led through to it, one by one. But to have the women turn on the Countess and vent their rage is an example of Borowczyk's genius for drama. There are psychological insights here, which go beyond language.

Maybe Walerian Borowczyk and his team are making a statement about how victims unconsciously go along with their oppressors, a truly depressing thought. Maybe there are equivalents to be made here with Poland under Communist rule, or other countries with oppressive regimes. The tropes of exploitation can be applied anywhere.

The *Erzsébet Báthory* episode is a mythical, dream-like sequence, and not meant to 'real' or 'literal', but if you look at the characters in it, there are only two people in that big, red room and twenty-five women, who could easily overpower them (thus, the scene also evokes a deeply disturbing element of exploitation and coercion – the collusion of the victims with their oppressors, their fatal masochism). But instead of overpowering Báthory and Istvan and escaping, the women turn from shredding Báthory's clothes to attacking each other. They revert to some primal, animal state, losing their humanity, and tearing at each other.

The chaos abruptly ends, the women disappear, and

14 This was rumoured to be performed by porn star Marie Forsa. It recalls the use of money in *La Marge* and *Ars Amandi*.
15 Reversing the gender, with a male Dracula faced with a room of women, wouldn't be nearly so compelling.

the Countess is alone once more with her page Istvan. The next cut is one of the most outrageous in Walerian Borowczyk's cinema, a supreme example of the power of editing: from the frenzy of the women the film cuts to two incredible close-ups: a big close-up of Báthory and a C.U. of the red pool. (This was apparently real blood – pigs' blood, because the filmmakers decided that fake blood wouldn't work. Perfectionist filmmakers have grappled with the problem of developing red stuff that looks convincingly like blood on screen. It's the wrong colour, wrong consistency, etc. It's also a tall order having to come up with gallons of it.)[16]

The Countess, naked, climbs into her bath and begins to wash herself with the blood of the dead women. Rather than the horror of the scene, the 1974 film concentrates on the painterly aspects of the red blood clinging in bubbles and swirls to Báthory's breasts, belly, buttocks and vulva. As in the previous episodes, the camera lingers in close-up on the woman's naked body.

It is a truly obscene sight – Countess Báthory bathing in the blood of twenty-five women. It's a literal bloodbath. The film calmly washes over the mechanics (and horror) of extermination, and focusses on the pleasure the Countess gleans from her bloodbath. (According to legend, the real Báthory was afraid of ageing, and bathed in blood for youth).

Isn't it a marvellous idea of the filmmakers to have Paloma Picasso play this mass murderer with a quiet, dignified (or indifferent) charm? One can imagine many another filmmaker and actor being unable to resist an obscene leer or two, a lick of the lips, some evil-eyed stare, or some other Movie Villain Business. But there's nothing at all: Báthory just goes about her bathing as if it's the most normal thing in the world. It's as if she's been doing it everyday. So the viewer supplies the horror. It might be a scented bubble bath bought from an exclusive boutique in Paris. (A Hollywood film would no doubt add some narrative elements like Báthory doing all

16 Some actresses might require some persuasion to bathe fully naked in real blood, but Picasso goes for it.

this because she is immortal, or long-lived, like Dracula. And Hollywood would no doubt design the Báthory mansion as a world of shadows and disturbing images, but *Erzsébet Báthory* resists all of that: it's all brightly lit).

But the movie stages it with a quiet reserve, all nice manners and people going about their business. And instead of major theatrics, *Immoral Tales* simply closes the scene in the bathroom with a close-up on the metal lid of the bath. No shots of the blood being flushed away down the drain. Having Báthory simply step out of the bath after the shower has washed off the blood and walk away is a deft way of depicting her complete detachment from what she has done. She is the calmest Bluebeard in cinema. (But here, finally, there is some emotional response from the perpetrators, when Istvan is depicted grimacing, and also expressing his/ her weariness. We can guess that it was Istvan who oversaw the mass murder of the women).

✻

The *Erzsébet Báthory* episode is the longest episode in *Immoral Tales* (at around 35 minutes); so, instead of ending here, with Countess Dracula bathing in women's blood, *Contes Immoraux* continues: the Countess climbs out of the bath, aided by her page Istvan; they retire to the blood-red, inner boudoir.

Some exquisite music opens the next scene in this incredible episode. It is a lesbian scene of sex and marriage. It's played entirely without dialogue, and it's rapt stuff.

Istvan is revealed, when she undresses, to be a young woman, and Báthory's lover. Báthory takes off Istvan's clothes, uncovering her slim form, and lets down her hair. The Countess quietly and lovingly dresses Istvan in a bridal outfit, putting a veil over her head. (Again, the movements of the women suggest that they have been enacting this rite for many a year).

The women, clad in diaphanous material through which their bodies are discernible, climb onto the bed and begin to make love. It's all very tender and graceful and gentle. The film captures the love-making with big close-ups of their naked bodies.

Erzsébet Báthory then cuts to some time later, the blood-red chamber now darkened. An elaborate master shot (a slow tilt, pan, zoom and tracking shot) shows the lovers lying beside each other (until Istvan wakes and quietly sneaks away).

The ending is swift: Istvan slips away from the bed. In the next shot, an officer enters the dark boudoir; Báthory wakes, startled; the officer informs the Countess that she is under arrest. Two guards come in and wrap the Countess in a black blanket and carry her off (an odd and inspired notion, as if she's too evil to be led away, and shouldn't be given the dignity of walking, or as if she's an animal and must be treated like something that must be taken out and thrown down a well or to the dogs, with suggestions of contamination, like the end of *Night of the Living Dead*, 1968).

In the final shot, Istvan is seen embracing the officer passionately; she loved him all along. Ah, bless! And the Countess gets her just desserts. Execution, presumably, after a rapid trial. (But not according to history, where Báthory was kept under house arrest). That Istvan is the worst sort of collaborator[17] is glossed over in favour of a smug embrace. (The clinch re-asserts the romantic, heterosexual couple at the heart of depictions of society in Western cinema. The kiss and the couple normalize everything we've seen, re-affirming conventional morality and the law).

---

17 Couldn't Istvan arrange to have the authorities turn up a few hours earlier?

Paloma Picasso in a superb costume by Piet Bolscher
in Immoral Tales

Who ordered the virgins' blood?
Immoral Tales

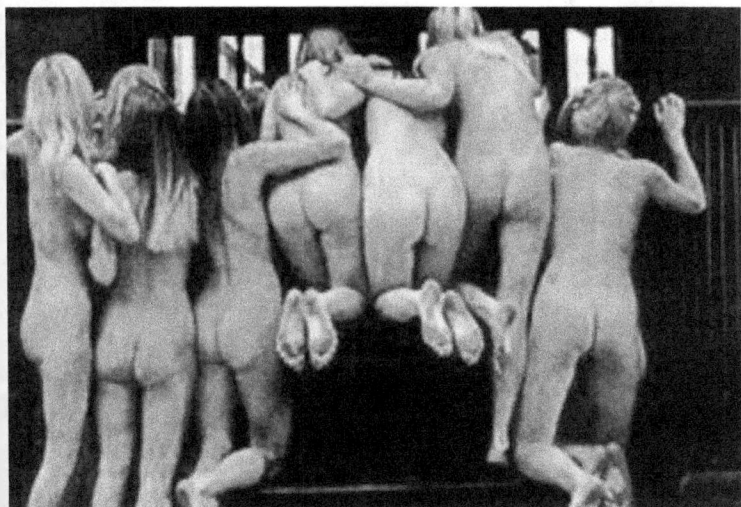

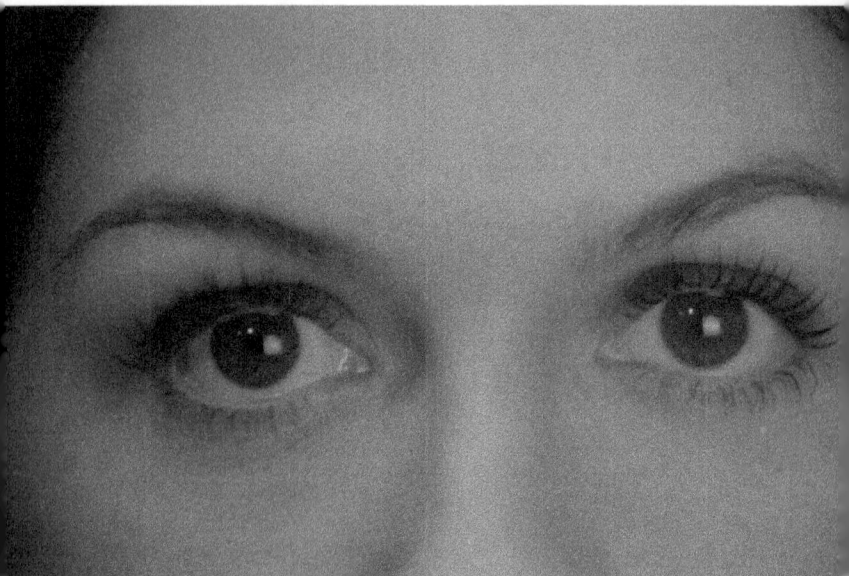

A Christopher Lee Dracula shot in Immoral Tales

Pascale Christophe in Immoral Tales

Some of the historical figures in Immoral Tales,
on this and the following pages:

Countess Báthory (16th century,
a copy of a lost painting)

"A glass of wine with Caesar Borgia", by J Collier (above).

Dosso Dossi, Lucrez Borgia, c. 1518, Melbourne (left).

LUCREZIA BORGIA

In the last episode of *Immoral Tales*, set in Italy in 1498, Lucrezia Borgia (Florence Bellamy) fools around with her brother Cesare Borgia, and their father, who's Pope Alexander VI (Mario Ruspoli, Borowczyk's friend, here using the moniker Jacopo Berinizi; Ruspoli's son Fabrizio played Cesare, under the name G. Lorenzo Berinizi). The *Borgias* episode has Lucrezia and her relatives cavorting in a white, Renaissance interior; the section culminates with group sex, with Lucrezia's brother Cesare tupping her from behind while she gives her father head (plus variations). It's a clichéd scene from pornography, but in Walerian Borowczyk's hands it becomes about something else – richer, stranger, and with a level of detail that pornography never has the time to construct. Aside from being a group sex scene, it's also graphic incest: a father having sex with his children. And he's the Pope!

And, like the *Erzsébet Báthory* episode, the *Lucrezia Borgia* episode also has a historical basis. In taking on the Borgias, *Immoral Tales* tackles one of the more notorious eras of Italian history. The *Borgias* sequence also combines sex and religion in a blasphemous whole.

The film takes place in the Vatican City primarily, with the Girolamo Savonarola (played by Philippe Desboeuf) scenes occurring in a church (primarily), and later in a square. Historically, Savonarola (1452-98) was Prior of San Marco in Florence, and was burned at the stake as a heretic in Piazza della Signoria, Firenze.

Lucrezia Borgia opens with a religious procession in the Vatican – the Pope, cardinals, a host of dignitaries, and the star of the piece, Lucrezia Borgia (Florence Bellamy), envisaged here as another of the young, slim, pale, dangerous *femme fatales* of Boro's cinema. It's a production value sequence, caught in a master shot which tracks and zooms in slowly, following the procession through a large, ornate doorway. The costumes are beautiful, and there's another lovely piece of Renaissance music.

Most of *Lucrezia Borgia* takes place within a single

chamber in the Vatican, another classic example of Walerian Borowczykian art direction: white marble walls and deep red hangings. Statues and busts. Religious ornaments. A white bench (which also resembles an altar). It was filmed in a studio in Sweden.

There are four people in the room: the three Borgias, and Lucrezia's husband, Giovanni Sforza. Fairly soon the Borgias are up to no good: they pull out some drawings and paintings of horses, with members prominent. These amuse the Borgias, especially father and daughter, for some time. Lucrezia's light but scornful laugh becomes one of the signature sounds of this episode in *Immoral Tales*. Everything is amusing to her. (Comic horse sounds are added to the movie, foreshadowing *The Beast* the following year).

Giovanni Sforza doesn't want to be part of this lewdness (which reflects history). And before long, he is taken away on the orders of the Pope – soldiers appear abruptly from a sliding wall behind a bust on a plinth (there are also bizarre insert shots, like a friar clearing up the horse drawings, and also the things the man's left behind, as if the papal chamber must remain spotless at all times, and all traces of Sforza must be erased).

Lucrezia Borgia is in her element, laughing with delight as she holds two drawings of a horse's penis against a wall, flicking between the two so it becomes erect (another animation idea – it's something that animators are always doing, to check the flow of movement). The film portrays an atmosphere of erotic pleasure which increases in stages. In one shot, Cesare, clad in scarlet, cardinal robes, is masturbating under his robes, stroking an erection.

When the 1974 film cuts to Girolamo Savonarola in Firenze, he is declaiming in a church pulpit, castigating the congregation for the wicked, debauched ways of the country. The crowd is heard but not seen; occasionally they shout at Savonarola and he responds to their cries. The off-screen sounds of people suggest a tumultuous historical period (the Savonarola section of *Immoral Tales* has a cheapo flavour – it isn't the most inventive way of circumventing a low budget. Also, as the final segment in the movie, some more money could've usefully been spent here).

Back in the Capital of Catholicism, the orgy begins. Lucrezia B. is very much the centre of it, with the action staged around her and with her body usually centre frame. With her father the Pope and her brother Cesare on either side of her, she kisses them and they begin to undress her. The camera lingers – for a *long* time – over close-ups of fingers undoing buttons, tilting down to show the dress gradually slipping to Lucrezia's ankles, then back up to her torso and naked breasts. The fetishistic delight in clothing is palpable (and it is a *fabulous* green dress). For costume designer Piet Bolscher such moments must be very gratifying, because his work is on show to an incredibly detailed degree. Borowczyk really knows how to photograph costumes.

Exquisite choral music plays throughout much of the *Lucrezia Borgia* episode.[1] The Pope is often declaiming too (the film is in French and Italian), so part of the episode is narrated, but Lucrezia's light, wry laughter cuts through all.

When Lucrezia Borgia is naked, she puts on a gown and stands on a chair, like a statue to be admired. Pope Alexander VI (apostrophizing her in religious terms) takes up a long, peacock's feather and plays it over Lucrezia's body, with close-ups of the feather brushing over Lucrezia's pussy. These erotic games are unusual enough in a movie, but when you remember that it's the Pope and his daughter and son, it becomes wickedly ironic. (And the camera is lingering here far longer than dramatically or thematically necessary).

Back in the Florentine church, Girolamo Savonarola's diatribe against the debauchery and lasciviousness of Italy becomes more incensed. No need to remark upon the montage structure Walerian Borowczyk is deploying here, in cutting from an incestuous orgy at the top of the power structure in Renaissance Italy and the

---

[1] Some of the sound mixing is patchy, or maybe the prints are now old.

San Marco Prior ranting in a church about declining morality. The movie is being outrageous, and Borowczyk knows it; and yet he can also say: well, it all really happened. And he can also say: there was much worse than this, which I haven't filmed, or wouldn't be allowed to film. (But for many viewers, this would already be way, way too much).

When the 1974 picture cuts back to the Vatican room, Lucrezia is being tupped from the rear by her brother Cesare. She's bent over the bench, face-down, loving it. Dad gets in on the action by climbing onto the bench and encouraging Lucrezia to service him.

When the Borgias change around, Lucrezia, nude, lies back on the bench with her arms outstretched: she is a naked crucifixion, a wholly secular – and sexual – mockery of Christian iconography. Her father climbs on top of her and fucks her.

When the film cuts again to Savonarola in the church, a couple of soldiers enter the scene, to drag him away for punishment. The Prior is still urging the crowd to repent as he's hauled off.

One of the most outrageous cuts in Walerian Borowczyk's cinema (and therefore in much of contemporary cinema) occurs next. It's a truly, mightily wild juxtaposition: from Savonarola burning at the stake in a square, surrounded by flames and smoke, to a huge close-up of Lucrezia's cunt (yes, that dreaded c-word – which evokes the brutality of the contrast).

If you wanted an example of Walerian Borowczyk at his blasphemous, outlandish best (or worst!), it's right here. The images – of Savonarola burning as a heretic at the stake and Lucrezia Borgia's vagina – are extreme enough, but to put them together like that is incredible. (And it's not a wide shot of Lucrezia, or a shot framing her torso, which would do just as well, but a big close-up of the woman's part).

As the camera pans around the half-naked bodies of the Pope and Cesare, with the nude Lucrezia lying between them in the afterglow of orgasm, *Immoral Tales* has reached an extraordinary climax. But it doesn't stop there. The filmmakers want to rub in the hypocrisy of Renaissance Italy even further, adding a *dénouement* of strangeness: in the coda, the Pope, cardinals, bishops and dignitaries have gathered to perform and witness the baptism of a baby (presumably it's either the Pope's child, or it's Cesare's child). The threesome of Pope, Cesare and Lucrezia is at the centre of this *tableau* of Happy Borgias. The setting is the doorway of the procession of the episode's beginning (and as indicated by the baby, presumably some months later).

The 1974 film cuts to big close-ups of the baby, smiling into the camera: the shot provides the final image of *Immoral Tales*. Do we need to state that this is a parody of the Nativity? (adding further layers of blasphemy). When the title card 'FIN' comes up, it's the end of one of the strangest films ever made.

Wow.

✳

If you take everything together that's depicted in *Immoral Tales*, you have one of the most mind-boggling movies of recent times. There are scenes here which, once seen, are never forgotten. Who else would make a twenty minute film of a young woman discovering masturbation, encouraged by the voice of God? Or a film of 'Countess Dracula' slaughtering twenty-five naked virgins, staged as a hypnotizing seduction of innocence by absolute evil? Or the tide timetables being used as an excuse for getting head in the surf? Or the Borgias, father, daughter and brother, having an orgy while Girolamo Savonarola burns at the stake?

Immoral Tales focusses on costumes to a fetishistic degree,
and includes some Parisian high fashion (and elaborate hats).
Piet Bolscher was costume designer. .

Naughty Lucrezia Borgia in Immoral Tales

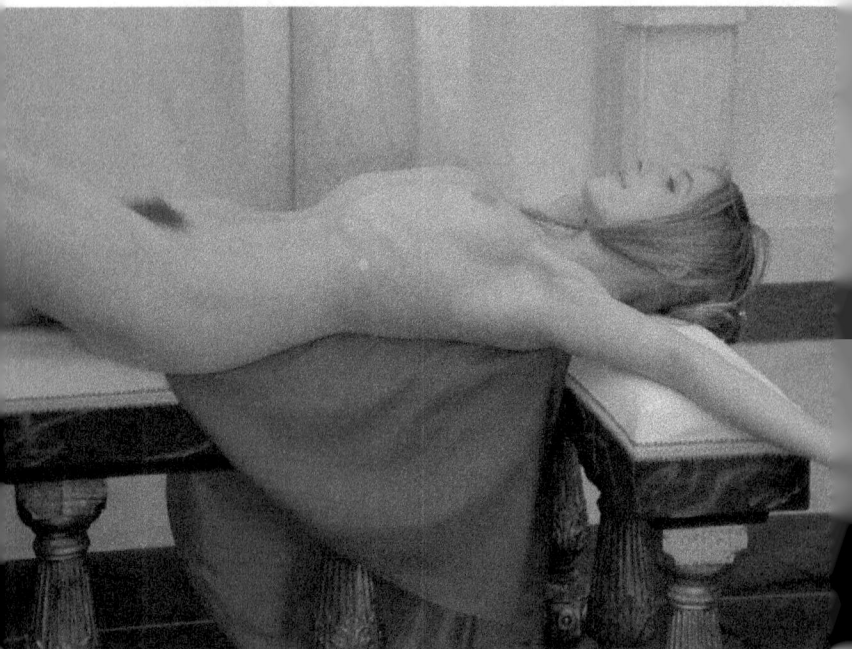

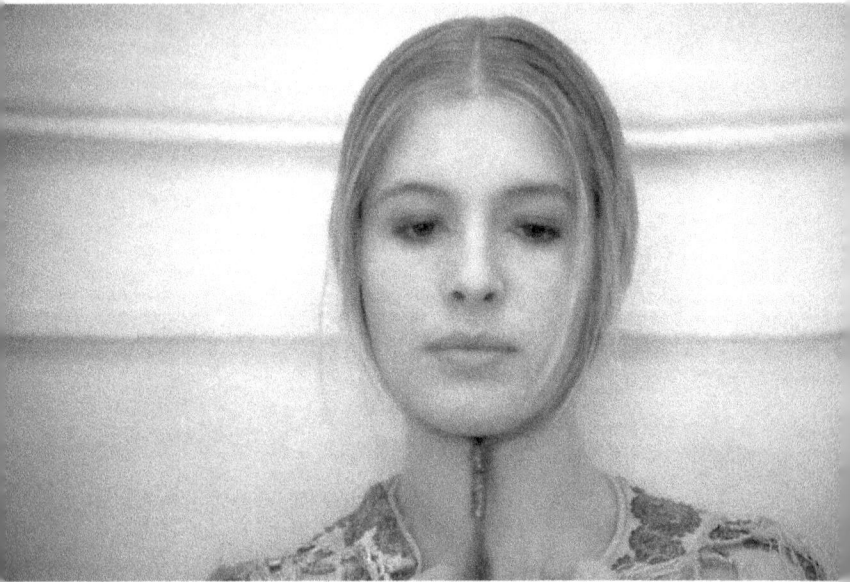

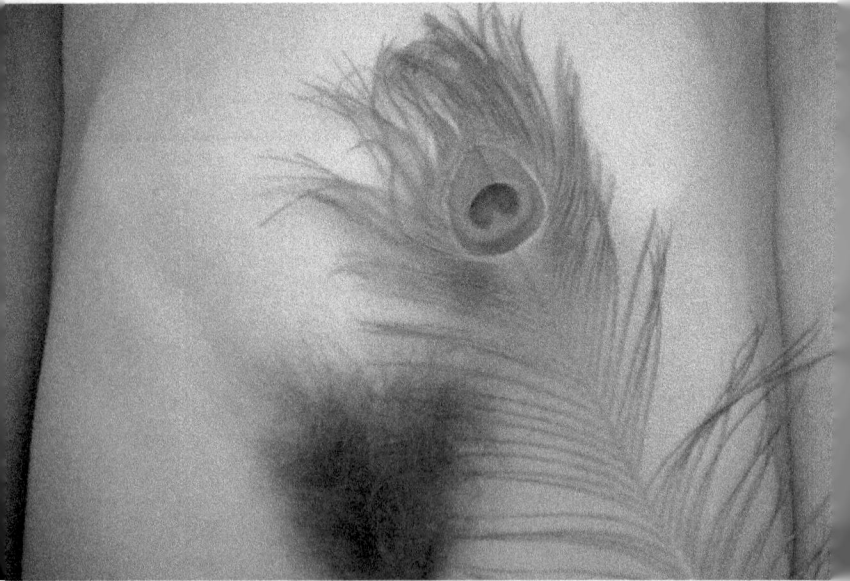

Savonarola (Philippe Desbeouf) in Immoral Tales (above).
Girolamo Savonarola, 1498, San Marco (below).

2

A PRIVATE COLLECTION
&
THE BEAST

Originally, *A Private Collection* was going to be part of *Immoral Tales* – it certainly acts as a diverting prologue. (It's a perfect introduction to Boro's erotic movies, and could play before *The Beast* or *The Art of Love*).

A Private Collection (*Une Collection Particulière*, 1973) was an amusing and playful exploration of a host of erotica, including sex toys, dildoes, prints, photographs, sculptures, automata, puppets, dolls, animation, magic lantern slides, and paintings. André Pieyre de Mandiargues, Boro's friend and artistic collaborator, narrated and starred in *A Private Collection*. It was produced by Anatole Dauman and P. Schamoni. 12 mins.

Une Collection Particulière comes across as the work of two 20th century libertines and connoisseurs of erotica transplanted from late 18th century Paris showing us around their Erotic Museums (you can visit Erotic Museums in Paris, Gotham, Amsterdam, etc, filled with similar paraphernalia).

The erotic prints and paintings in *A Private Collection* include some of the usual suspects from the history of erotic art – such as Peter Fendi and Rembrandt van Rijn, along with many anonymous photographs from the late 19th and early 20th centuries.[1] (Some of these pop up in Borowczyk's cinema, along with the *objéts d'art*).

There are some early devices designed to titillate in *Une Collection Particulière* – wooden models and automata (such as a policeman getting an erection, a man doing a donkey, and silhouettes of people tupping). Some of these quaint machines pre-date cinema, but simulate movement and life, and're part of Walerian Borowczyk's fascination with animation, and animating the inanimate, which was such a large ingredient of Borowczyk's early films. (Some of the objects were made by Boro, and crafted to look aged).

The early animated film strips in *A Private Collection* are precursors of modern cel animation, but

1 De Mandiargues' finger covers up the genitals.

the scenes they depict (including bestiality), are not your usual animated fare (!).[2] *A Private Collection* is fascinated with the mechanics of producing these images and film strips, using old film projectors and magic lanterns. (Some of the strips are hand-tinted, and several feature magic acts and circuses, reminding us of the origins of cinema in the culture of funfairs and circuses).

The erotic sculptures and automata displayed in *A Private Collection* are mainly wooden, painted, and of course handmade (some of the objects that Borowczyk built in his own art practice echo these sculptures). Some of them are delightful objects, with the homespun charm of outsider art and amateur art. It's the sense of humour, the ridiculousness of sex, that comes across (the wry commentary by André Pieyre de Mandiargues points us in that direction, of course. In one scene, he mimes masturbation with a dildo and a mirror, as if the audience couldn't figure out how to do it. The act pops up in *Behind Convent Walls*).

Sex toys are another part of *A Private Collection* (it's amazing how much erotic bric-a-brac de Mandiargues and Boro manage to squeeze into twelve minutes): assorted dildoes (complete with their own wooden, storage boxes, so they sit on the shelf quite innocently), and also a dildo with a face painted on the end (a similar sex toy was employed in *Behind Convent Walls*).

A Private Collection also exhibits Boro's fascination with early forms of technology – of suggesting movement, and of recording sound. Prior to 1895 and the Lumière Brothers, plenty of devices existed to suggest motion (any film or TV or science museum displays them). It was inevitable that depicting sex acts would be included in the content of early cinematic technology.

The soundtrack of *A Private Collection*, meanwhile, is a selection of Boro's rare recordings (played on what appears to be the phonograph from the 1969 short film). In a typically eccentric gesture, the soundtrack also

2 They demonstrate that as soon as new technologies are invented, pornography and exploitation get in there very rapidly.

includes the sound of the needle reaching the end of the play-out groove, and repeating...

THE BEAST

The story of *La Bête* (a.k.a. *The Beast, The Beast In Heat* and *Death's Ecstasy*, 1975) drew on the legend, myth and history of the Beast of Gévaudan,[3] which has been the subject of documentaries: History Channel (2009), natural history shows, etc, several books, TV films (French, 2003), *Teen Wolf* (M.T.V.), and other movies (French, 2001).

Among the crew on *La Bête* were DPs Bernard Daillencourt and Marcel Grignon, Noël Véry, camera operator, Jacques D'Ovidio, production designer, set decorator Alain Guillé, wardrobe by Piet Bolscher, make-up by Odette Berroyer, production manager Dominique Duvergé and sound by Michel Laurent and Jean-Pierre Ruh (sound mixer was Alex Pront). No less than six assistant editors are credited (Alain Cayrade, Florence Dauman,[4] Claude Delon, Jean-Pierre Platel, Monique Prim and Michel Valio – some were trainees), but it's Boro who has the main editing credit. Many on the team were regulars in the Borowczyk Travelling Circus. Eastmancolor. 93 minutes (*The Beast* is 2,837 metres/ 9,220 feet long).[5]

The chateau in the film is Chateau de Nandy, 25 miles from Paris; it has been used many times for movies

3 On the beast of Gévaudan, see: P. Pourcher, *The Beast of Gevaudan,* tr. by D. Brockis, Author House, 2006; J. Smith, *Monsters of the Gévaudan,* Harvard University Press, Cambridge, MA, 2011; R. Thompson, *Wolf-Hunting In France In the Reign of Louis XV: The Beast of the Gévaudan,* 1991; M. Louis, *La Bête Du Gévaudan – L'innocence Des Loups,* Librairie Académique Perrin, 2001; F. Fabre, *La bête du Gévaudan, Edition complétée par Jean Richard,* Editions De Boré, 2002. Also: the website www.betedugevaudan.com.
4 Producer Dauman's daughter.
5 *The Beast* was released in the U.S.A. in 1977 (in a 98-minute version).

and TV (including *Arsène Lupin*, 2004, *The Aristos*, 2006, and *Le Retour du Héroes*, 2018).

One of the sources of *La Bête* was an 18th century French fable, *La véritable histoire de la bête de Gévaudin* (which Walerian Borowczyk had turned into an 18-minute short in 1973, entitled *La véritable histoire de la bête du Gévaudan*; it was shown as a work-in-progress at the London Film Festival, comprising the last of three self-contained films in *Immoral Tales*). Another was a movie that Borowczyk was hired to work on, *Les rendezvous en forêt*, directed by Alain Fleischer. Producer Anatole Dauman wanted Borowczyk to spice up the ending, and Boro constructed a beast suit.[6] However, Fleischer prevented Borowczyk from adding to *Les rendezvous en forêt* through legal action, and Borowczyk would later use his beast costume in *La Bête* (a costume in search of a film, then – very Borowczykian!). *La Bête* also, unlike too many of Borowczyk's other films, is not dubbed (or a large proportion of the movie has source sound).[7] There's a greater sense of performance and atmosphere.

The 1975 movie jettisons many of the aspects of the Beast of Gévaudan legend, but it does retain the notion of a strange creature terrorizing the region, the preying upon solitary figures (such as shepherdesses), and the idea that someone with social power was controlling it.

To the legend of the Beast, the 1975 feature-length version added a story which involves a North American heiress Lucy Broadhurst[8] (Lisbeth Hummel) being brought to a French chateau with her Aunt Virginia (Elisabeth Kaza) by the scheming owners (in particular the Marquis, Pierre de l'Esperance, played by Guy Tréjan), who need to marry her to the earthy, degenerate (and somewhat backward) son of the family, Mathurin (Pierre Benedetti) in order to circumvent a will which'll keep the family home intact.

6 The Beast has gorilla hands and a wolf head, and black hair all over. Borowczyk himself played the Beast. Nah, just kidding.
7 The short film was shot wild, and is looped.
8 Lucy is young, blonde, and wears a huge, expensive fur coat (another of many beastly motifs in *La Bête*). Lucy is depicted as a naïve, innocent (and rather dim) soul.

That's the framing story of *The Beast*, about grasping aristocrats, decadent morality, degenerate priests and sexually repressed young women.9 This part of the film's set in the 20th century, though it's not the conventional modern, urban world of many movies. *La Bête* takes place exclusively at the French chateau and its grounds (the film is in French, but there is English dialogue – Virginia, Lucy and their chauffeur speak English – tho' not all of them with convincing American accents).

There are subplots woven into the main narrative of *The Beast* of the imminent marriage of Lucy and Mathurin: the Cardinal Joseph de Balo, brother of the Marquis's uncle, the disabled Duc de Balo (Marcel Dalio), who's supposed to come to the chateau to perform the wedding ceremony, but has fallen out with him;10 the telephone calls to the Vatican, trying to persuade him to visit; the Marquis, Pierre de l'Esperance, who's orchestrating the marriage; the uncouth Mathurin, who's happiest outside with his horses and is terrified of being married off (he has a bandaged hand, which's part of his Beast nature); the Priest (Roland Armontel) with his pretty choirboys who follow him around meekly (one is called Modeste,11 played by Thierry Bourdone);12 the black man servant Ifany (Hassane Fall) who sneaks off to make the beast with two backs with the Marquis's daughter, Clarisse de l'Esperance (Pascale Rivault); and two children, friends of the Marquis's daughter, who've come to witness the wedding.

There are three romantic/ erotic liaisons in *The Beast*:

  ✳ Lucy and Mathurin and their nuptials
  ✳ Romilda and the Beast

9 Borowczyk said he had written *La Bête* in two days, and had the initial idea in a café (of course – he was living in Paris, cafés being crucibles of many a creative venture).

10 The Marquis uses blackmail to persuade the Duke to ask his brother the Cardinal to come to bless the marriage (the Marquis claims that the Duke poisoned his wife).

11 Modeste because of Modest Mussorgsky perhaps? Or Modest, the gay brother of the gay Peter Tchaikovsky?

12 It's the choirboys who play the harpsichord, which justifies the use of the music within the movie (and Thierry Bourdone is better at miming playing than Sirpa Lane.

✳ Clarisse and Ifany

The key romantic relationship in the present day, the arranged marriage, is linked to issues such as economics, status, class, heredity, religion and parents vs. children. Dramatically, simple pairs or opposites are evoked:

Marquis	Mathurin
Marquis	Duke
Lucy	Mathurin
Virginia	Marquis

Tying most of the plots and subplots together in *The Beast* is not Lucy or Mathurin, but the Marquis: to him, many of the plots are linked, including the marriage plot, the Clarisse and Ifany subplot, the Priest and his sidekicks plot, the conflict with the Duke of Balo plot, etc.

In addition, *The Beast* presents several pairs of issues:

religion	paganism
civilization	nature
repression	freedom/ sex
indoors	outside
present	past
patriarchy	femininity
parents	children

The Beast links the two stories with sex – and with masturbation in particular. Thus, the other main narrative in *The Beast* depicts Lucy's masturbatory fantasies of erotic encounters with a Beast in a sunlit forest, set in the 18th century, imagining (or remembering) herself as Romilda de l'Esperance (played by Sirpa Lane, 1951-99), one of the ancestors of the Marquis's family, meeting the legendary Beast that has haunted the family for centuries (the legend is that a Beast emerges every two hundred years in the park). (Sirpa Lane had a short film career before she died of AIDS in 1999. *The Beast* was her third or fourth movie, and most of her work was in exploitation or underground cinema. She was 24 when *The Beast* was filmed.)

Walerian Borowczyk, 52 when it was released, called *The Beast* 'really more of a comedy than an erotic film'. Let that prepare you for this extraordinary movie. Because the central section, the fairy tale sequence of the Beast pursuing and fucking a woman, is meant to be very silly, very over-the-top, very unbelievable. *The Beast is* a comedy, and it *is* erotic. And it's so completely mad you can't help but be swept along by it. Have a look at some of the comments on the Internet Movie Database and Amazon for some funny takes on the movie. (So, no need for a spoof or parody of *The Beast* by Mel Brooks or Zucker-Abrahams-Zucker[3] because it already contains send-ups of itself, and of Boro's cinema).

Walerian Borowczyk remarked that:

> *La Bête* is a fantasy film and especially an 'adult film'. But first of all it is a film about dream mechanisms. Dreams translate our deepest desires. Why then cover with a veil of silence the temptation of an intimate relationship with an animal? (J. Gerber, 169)

Walerian Borowczyk here outlines one of his central goals – which is to make manifest desires and fears that are hidden or suppressed (he's especially fond of exposing them within a religious/ Catholic context, partly because the desires, when they erupt, appear even more out-rageous. Organized religion is a great environment against which to set explosions of desire, as artists have known for millennia. It's a rich context for horror movies, and for comedy, too, for the same reasons – authority figures, taboos, hierarchies, rules, etc. To show something wild, place it against something repressed, restrained, conservative, traditional, etc).

The 'controversy' surrounding *The Beast* from its release onwards pivoted on the fantasy scenes of Romilda de l'Esperance having sex with 'the Beast'. There were the inevitable run-ins with censors and the media. *La Bête* retained its power to upset viewers, even shock, many years later. In Britain, the British Board of Film

---

13 I would like to see them take on *The Beast!*

Classification could not pass it; in 1978 it was granted an 'X' by the Greater London Council (and only after extensive cuts), and was only allowed to be seen in London (and only with armed police present, just in case the outraged audience rioted). It was not granted a certificate by the B.B.F.C. in Albion until 2001, due to the relaxation of censorship laws, turning up on video, DVD and the FilmFour TV channel.

La Bête finally enters the famous sequence of the monster and the woman, Romilda (around the 55 minute mark): it's framed as Lucy's dream or memory or fantasy: she is lying back on her bed, in her gauzy, white gown, holding the red rose. The past, two hundred years earlier, is a cultured world of Domenico Scarlatti music – Romilda is first seen playing it in the chateau on a sunny, Summer's day (every time *The Beast* cuts back to the forest sequence, the Scarlatti music is pounding away. Why does the harpsichord sound so much heavier than the regular grand piano? (Or even a heavy rock band?) The music begins as kind of diegetic, but it continues throughout the sequence, long after Romilda has abandoned the harpsichord in the villa for a romp in the woodland).

The version of *The Beast* filmed in 1973, when it was going to be one of several shorts collected as *Immoral Tales*, doesn't rattle through the film projector in the 1975 version of *The Beast* until some 55 minutes into the show. Why? One obvious reason is that the footage is so over-the-top, it can only play towards the end of the movie. You can't follow it. You can't have the bestial rape fantasy first and then shift into an hour of seedy aristos yakking in drawing rooms.

This is, after all, one of the selling points of *The Beast* (as the producers and distributors knew well – look at the marketing, for example, which emphasizes the Sirpa Lane/ Beast encounter). And you don't give the whole thing away in the first five minutes (rather, you tease the audience).

A key decision was to cut up the 1973 version of *La Bête*: you could have Lucy dreaming then cut to the fantasy playing all the way through. By moving back and forth, *The Beast* now presents the past and the present day commenting upon and modulating each other: there are two young maidens and two Beasts, two sex acts, two deaths (in the present day, though, the gender roles are reversed, so it's the woman who is the active one, the predator sneaking into the beloved's room, stroking his body).

Once the decision's been made to cut up the 1973 *Beast* into sections, the next issue is: *when* to cut back and forth? One time-switch occurs between the imagery of the sacrificed lamb in the past and the murder of Duc de Balo in the present (so who is the true Beast? The Marquis, perhaps – he kills in cold blood. When it comes to real vicious, psychotic behaviour, animals aren't a patch on humans. Indeed – the Beast itself is slain by Romilda in the past).

The first time that Romilda sees the Beast is when she finds the bloody remains of the lamb on the ground, and the Beast is nearby. The sight of the corpse and the blood trigger off the hysterical section of this mad version of *Little Red Riding Hood* meets *Beauty and the Beast* meets arty Euro-erotica. (As everything in this part of *The Beast* is completely preposterous, Sirpa Lane performs several eye-popping reaction shots in the silent-era manner).

The last of the sex scenes between Romilda de l'Esperance and *la bête* in the woodland occur straight after the remarkable extreme close-up of Lucy masturbating with a red rose. The Beast grapples the woman onto a tree trunk and begins to take her from behind. Close-ups of his penis, his balls, her buttocks, her face (the editing becomes rapid and fragmentary). Romilda seems to swoon away from the intensity of the experience. Then she returns to consciousness (expressed with a close-up of her hand, resting on top of her white dress, which begins to move with the rhythm of the Beast's movements), and she starts to enjoy what's happening (her gasps are loud, and she licks her lips lasciviously – a classic, Borowczykian touch).

The tempo of the cutting increases, as the love-making reaches a climax, which occurs with a money shot, a close-up of the Beast coming over the woman's rear (one of many orgasms the Beast has). Lucy is on the bed back in the present day, continuing to masturbate (with the white dress drawn between her thighs). In Boro's cinema, once aroused, erotic *jouissance*, particularly in women, assumes an unstoppable vigour. Borowczyk's films find sex ridiculous, sad, coercive and manipulative, but also awe-inspiring: look, humans can do *that*.

The 1975 film then ascends to a plateau of orgasmic pleasures, as the woman and the Beast are seen enjoying a variety of sexual acts. Romilda isn't running away now – she becomes assertive, throwing off her clothing, and leading the scene: here's Romilda squeezing her breasts and nipples to tantalize the Beast... the Beast fucking her breasts... copious amounts of sperm dripping over her body, down to her vulva... Romilda putting her fingers inside herself from the rear... Romilda rubbing the animals's weenie all over her face... Romilda licking the Beast's penis as she straddles him... Romilda jerking him with her feet, and so on.

It's Boro's version of the *Kama Sutra*, or Agostino Carracci's *I Modi* (*The Ways*), as Romilda uses her mouth, hands, feet, breasts, hair, ass, vulva and anything else she can think of to get the Beast off. (Gangster/ thriller movies just need 'a girl and a gun' – Borowczyk prefers 'a girl and a beast'... or 'a girl and a room with hidden erotica').

Down on the ground, Romilda masturbates *la bête*, and licks him again, and he dies (there's blood around his muzzle). There's a final roar, and the Domenico Scarlatti music falls away. It's an ecstasy (the 'death's ecstasy' of one of the film's many alternative titles). And that, of course, is one of the recurring fantasies of Western literature. And it's very Surrealist and Sadeian, too: dying at orgasm. (One can imagine the Marquis de Sade enjoying every minute of *The Beast*).

During the sex scenes with the creature, *The Beast*

doesn't just concentrate on genitals contacting each other, or to close-ups of parts of the eroticized body, as in conventional pornography, it cuts away, many times, to images of the trees and bushes, to a white cloth with blood on it, and to the progress of a snail crawling over Romilda's shoe (the snail, one of many creatures in *La Bête*, is obviously a symbol of phallic/ erotic fecundity: the snail and the shoe feature prominently when the Beast is fucking Romilda from the rear – she stares at it. A phallic snail, a vaginal shoe. The snail and shoe fall to the ground symbolically, just as the Beast dies in a series of rapid cuts). *The Beast* also employs subjective shots of Romilda's views of the forest as she's being taken: the forest floor, the trees above, with the camera swinging back and forth to simulate the rhythms of sex.[14]

There is a lot to *The Beast*, once you get beyond the sheer silliness of it all. On a script and narrative level, *The Beast* is actually cleverly worked out (including how the fantasy story two hundred years ago impacts on the present day story. There are numerous rhymes and echoes which are all planned at the script stage). And while the monster suit and the chase are pure pantomime or vaudeville, there are some impressive technical effects in *The Beast*, but many of them are invisible: the editing, for a start (courtesy of the maestro and an army of editorial assistants). Nearly always the last thing viewers and critics comment upon in Walerian Borowczyk's cinema (hell, there's all that naked flesh to contemplate first), the editing in Borowczyk's films is virtuosic. It's as impressive as any of Borowczyk's contemporary European art filmmakers. Sure, Jean-Luc Godard or Ingmar Bergman are taken so seriously in other areas of filmmaking (politically, psychologically, socially), but at the level of editing and organizing material, Borowczyk is a magician. Just look at the way he and the assistants are bringing together all of the characters in *The Beast*.

---

14 Ken Russell used the same technique in *Women In Love* and *Valentino*.

A Private Collection (1973), this page and over.

The Beast, filmed in 1973 (and used as part of the 1975 version), this page and over.

The legend starts out on a beautiful Summer's day, with Romilda playing the harpsichord in a pale blue dress.

Beauty and the Beast, Borowczyk-style.

The filmmakers run thru the Kama Sutra and I Modi (The Ways) in The Beast

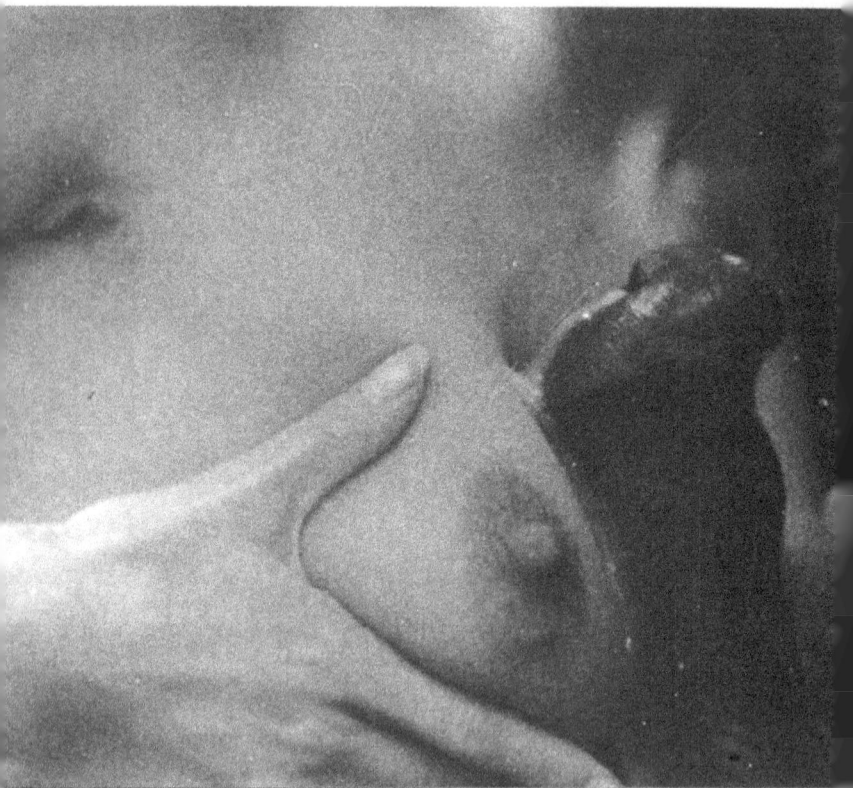

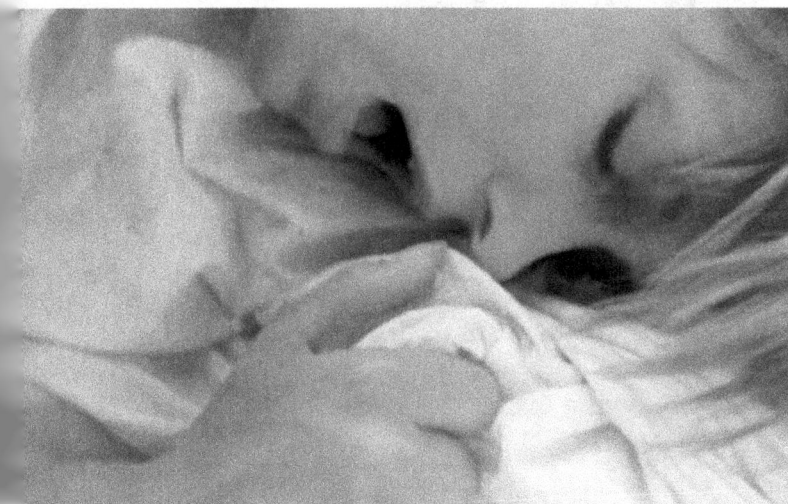

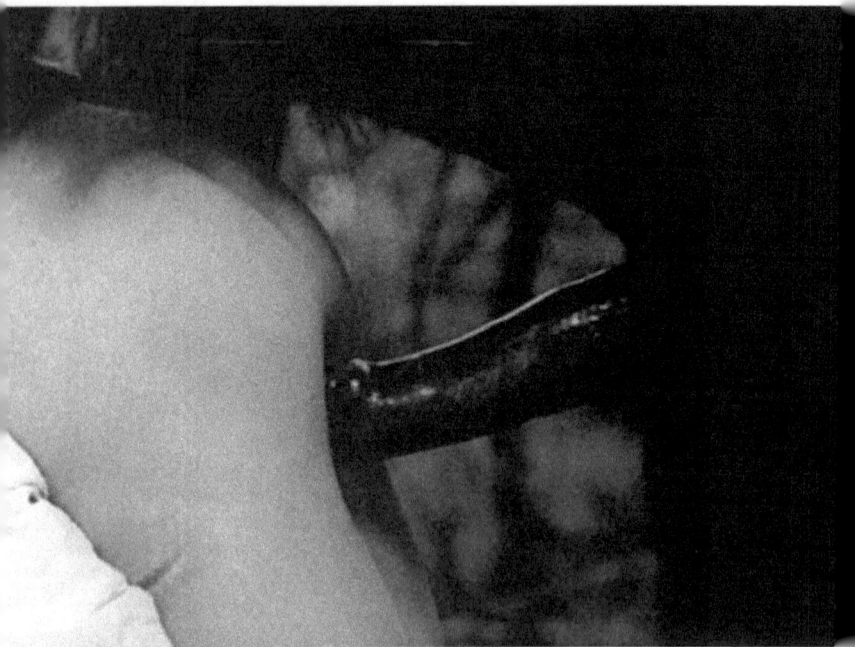

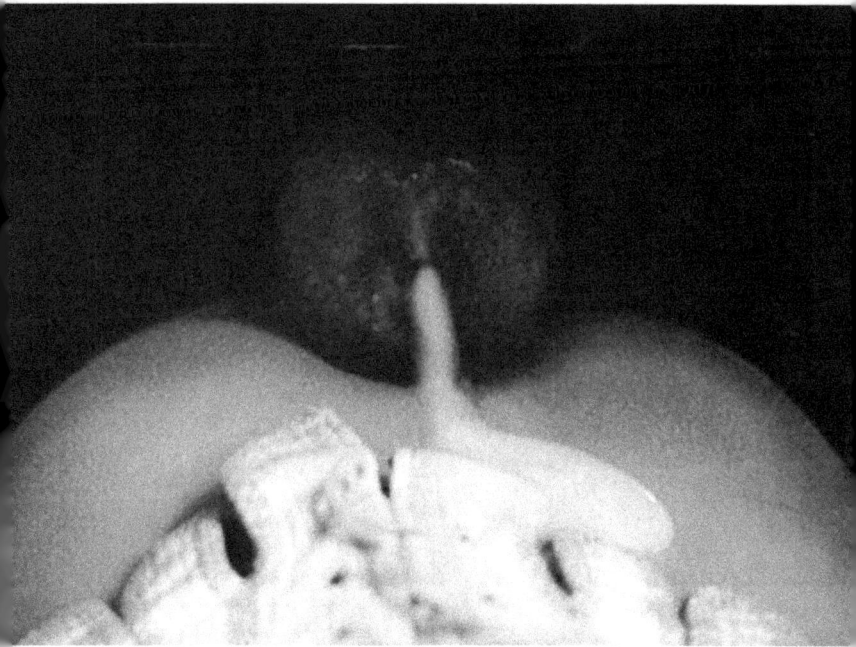

Walerian Borowczyk makes no apologies for bringing the subtext of a
movie out into the open in The Beast

APPENDICES

QUOTES BY
WALERIAN BOROWCZYK

All stages of a film's creation are in me at one and the same time. My temperament does not allow me to create only part of a work and then to entrust the rest to specialists... I... eliminate the collaborators who dare to try and barter my own ideas with me. *I know everything.* And that very often drives members of my crew to tears.

✤

I attach a great deal of importance to details

✤

I conceive all my films in an instant, and only objective means prevent me from making them in that instant.

✤

La Bête is a fantasy film and especially an 'adult film'. But first of all it is a film about dream mechanisms. Dreams translate our deepest desires. Why then cover with a veil of silence the temptation of an intimate relationship with an animal?

✤

If I have to choose an epoch and an identity, it would be that of Leda's swan in antiquity (if she really was as beautiful as the artists represent her).

✤

Eroticism, sex, is one of the most moral parts of life. Eroticism does not kill, exterminate, encourage evil, lead to crime. On the contrary, it makes people gentler, brings joy, gives fulfilment, leads to selfless pleasure.

FILMOGRAPHY

IMMORAL TALES

A.k.a. *Contes Immoraux*
Released: Aug 28, 1974. 105 mins.

CAST

Lise Danvers – Julie
Fabrice Luchini – André
Charlotte Alexandra – Thérèse
Paloma Picasso – Elisabeth Báthory
Pascale Christophe – Istvan
Florence Bellamy – Lucrezia Borgia
Jacopo Berinizi – Pope Alexander VI
G. Lorenzo Berinizi – Cesare Borgia
Philippe Desboeuf – Giralomo Savonarola
Marie Forså – Close-up girl
Robert Capia
Kjell Gustavsson
Tomas Hnevsa
Nicole Karen
Mathieu Rivollier
Gerard Tcherka

CREW

Producer – Anatole Dauman
Script – Walerian Borowczyk and André Pieyre de Mandiargues
Original Music – Maurice Le Roux
Cinematography – Bernard Daillencourt, Guy Durban, Noël Véry and Michel Zolat
Editing – Walerian Borowczyk and Anne-Marie Sachs
Production Design – Walerian Borowczyk
Costume Design – Piet Bolscher
Assistant Director – Dominique Duvergé
Production assistants – Alain Cayrade, Bernard Grignon, Maxine Groffsky, Alain Herpe and Jean-Pierre Platel

OTHER MOVIES DIRECTED BY WALERIAN BOROWCZYK

Mr. and Mrs. Kabal's Theatre (1967)
A.k.a. *Théâtre de M. et Mme. Kabal*
Producers – Jacques Forgeot and André G. Brunelin
Script – Walerian Borowczyk

Goto, Island of Love (1969)
A.k.a. *Goto, l'île d'amour*
Producers – Louis Duchesne and René Thévenet
Script – Walerian Borowczyk and Dominique
Duvergé

Blanche (1971)
Producers – Philippe d'Argila and Dominique
Duvergé
Script – Walerian Borowczyk
Story – *Mazepa* by Juliusz Slowacki

The Beast (1975)
A.k.a. *The Beast In Heat. The Beast. Death's Ecstasy*
Producer – Anatole Dauman
Script – Walerian Borowczyk

The Story of Sin (1975)
Script – Walerian Borowczyk
Story – the novel by Stefan Zeromski

La Marge (1976)

A.k.a. *Emmanuelle '77. The Margin. The Streetwalker*

    Producers   Raymond and Robert Hakim

    Script – Walerian Borowczyk

    Story – André Pieyre de Mandiargues' novel *The Margin*

Behind Convent Walls (1977)

A.k.a. *Interno di un convento. Sex Life in a Convent. Within a Cloister*

    Producer – Giuseppe Vezzani

    Script – Walerian Borowczyk

Three Immoral Women (1979)

A.k.a. *Heroines of Evil. Heroines of Pain. Immoral Women*

    Producers – Pierre Braunberger and Gisèle Braunberger

    Executive Producers – Jean-Paul de Vidas, Michel de Vidas

    Script – Walerian Borowczyk and André Pieyre de Mandiargues

Lulu (1980)

    Producers – Robert Kuperberg and Jean-Pierre Labrande

    Script – Walerian Borowczyk, Anton Giulio Majano and Géza von Radványi

Doctor Jeckyll and His Women (1981)

A.k.a. *Docteur Jekyll et les femmes. The Blood/bath of Doctor Jeckyll. Bloodlust. Dr. Jeckyll and Miss Osbourne. The Experiment*

    Producers – Ralph Baum, Robert Kuperberg and Jean-Pierre Labrande

    Script – Walerian Borowczyk

    Story – Robert Louis Stevenson's novel *The Strange Case of Dr. Jeckyll and Mr. Hyde*

The Art of Love (1983)
A.k.a. *Ars Amandi. L'arte di amare. L'Art d'aimer*
Executive Producer – Marcel Albertini
Producers – Mario Lupi, Camillo Teti and Ugo Tucci
Script – Walerian Borowczyk, Wilhelm Buchheim
and Enzo Ungari
Story – Ovid

Emmanuelle 5 (1987)
Producer – Alain Siritzky
Script – Walerian Borowczyk and Alex Cunningham

Love Rites (1987)
A.k.a. *Cérémonie d'amour. Queen of the Night.*
Rites of Love
Producers – Alain Sarde and Philippe Guez
Script – Walerian Borowczyk
Story – André Pieyre de Mandiargues' novel *Tout*
disparaitra

Softly From Paris (1986-1991)
A.k.a. *Série rose*, 26 episodes, 1986-1991.
Broadcast: FR3, RTL9 and NT1.
Production companies – Pierre Grimblat/ FR3/
Hamster Prods.
Executive Producers – Nicolas Traube, Michaëla
Watteaux and Gaspard de Chavagnac
Producer – Pierre Grimblat
Walerian Borowczyk directed four episodes: *Le lotus*
d'or (1986), *Un traitement mérité* (1990), *Almanach des*
adresses des demoiselles de Paris (1990) and *L'experte*
Halima (1991).
Sources – Giovanni Boccaccio, *The Decameron;*
Anonymous (1791); *Jin Ping Mei;* and the *1001 Nights.*
Scripts – Alain Schwarzstein, Patrick Pesnot, Yves
Belaure and Boro.

OTHER FILM PROJECTS DIRECTED BY WALERIAN BOROWCZYK

Mois d'août (1946)

Photographies vivantes (1954)

Studio of Fernand Léger (1954)

Autumn (a.k.a. *Jesien*, 1955)

Once Upon a Time (1957)

School (1958)

Requited Feelings (a.k.a. *Nagrodzone uczucia*, 1958)

House (1959)

The Astronauts (1959)

The Concert of M. et Mme. Kabal (1962)

The Encyclopedia of Grandmother (1963)

Holy Smoke (1963)

Renaissance (1964)

Angels' Games (1965)

Joachim's Dictionary (1965)

Rosalie (1966)

Diptych (1967)

Mr. and Mrs. Kabal's Theatre (a.k.a. *Théâtre de M. et Mme. Kabal*, 1967)

Gavotte (1968)

The Phonograph (1969)

A Private Collection (1973)

Letter From Paris (1975)

Escargot de Venus (1975)

The Greatest Love of All Times (1977)

Private Collections (1979), segment: *The Wardrobe*

Scherzo Infernal (1984)

BIBLIOGRAPHY

Sue Adler. "Enticements to Voyeurism", *Cinema Papers*, 50, Feb, 1985

D. Bird. *Boro, Walerian Borowczyk*, Le Chineur, 2017

D. Bond. *The Fiction of André Pieyre de Mandiargues*, Syracuse University Press, New York, 1982

W. Borowczyk. Interview with Andrzej Markowski, *Kino*, 4, 1975

—. *Anatomy of the Devil*, 1992

—. *My Polish Years*, Hypnos Media, Paris, 2001

Borowczyk: Cinéaste Onirique: Le cas étrange du Dr Jekyll et Miss Osbourne, Collection La Vue and B. Diffusion, Paris, 1981

D. Dourdet. *André Pieyre de Mandiargues*, Visages d'aujourd'hui, Paris, 1960

A. Carter. *The Virago Book of Fairy Tales*, Virago 1991

A. Castant. *Esthétique de l'image, fictions d'André Pieyre de Mandiargues*, Recifs, Sorbonne, Paris

S. Cohan & I.R. Hark, eds. *Screening the Male: Exploring Masculinities In Hollywood Cinema*, Routledge, London, 1993

D.A. Cook. *A History of Narrative Film*, W.W. Norton, New York, N.Y., 1981, 1990, 1996

B. Creed. "Horror and the Monstrous-Feminine: An Imaginary Abjection", *Screen*, 27, 1, 1985

—. "*Alien* and the Monstrous-Feminine", in A. Kuhn, 1990

—. "Dark Desires: Male Masochism and the Horror Film", in S. Cohan, 1993

—. *The Monstrous-Feminine*, Routledge, London, 1993

M. Crosland, ed. *The Marquis de Sade Reader*, Peter Owen, 2000

L. Doan, ed. *The Lesbian Postmodern*, Columbia University Press, New York, N.Y., 1994

J. Donald, ed. *Fantasy and the Cinema*, British Film Institute, London, 1989

Andrea Dworkin. *Intercourse*, Arrow, London, 1988

—. *Pornography: Men Possessing Women*, Women's Press, London, 1984

John Fletcher & Andrew Benjamin, eds. *Abjection, Melancholia and Love: the Work of Julia Kristeva*, Routledge, London, 1990

Lorraine Gamman & Margaret Marshment, eds. *The Female Gaze: Women as Viewers of Popular Culture*, Women's Press, London, 1988

J. Geiger & R. Rutsky, eds. *Film Analysis*, Norton & Company, New York, N.Y., 2005

J. Gerber. *Pierre Braunberger*, Pompidou, Paris, 1987

—. *Anatole Dauman: Pictures of a Producer*, British Film Institute, London, 1992

T. Gilliam. *Gilliam On Gilliam*, ed. I. Christie, Faber, London, 1999

D. Gras-Durosini. *Mandiargues et ses récits*, L'Harmattan, Paris, 2006

S. Grossman. *L'œil du poète: André Pieyre de Mandiargues et la peinture*, Lettres modernes-Minard, Paris, 1999

Elizabeth Grosz. "Irigaray and Sexual Difference", *Australian Feminist Studies*, 2, 1986

—. "Desire, the body and recent French feminism", *Intervention*, 21-2, 1988

—. *Sexual Subversions*, Allen & Unwin, London, 1989

—. "The Body of Signification", in J. Fletcher, 1990

—. "Lesbian Fetishism?", *differences*, 3, 2, 1991

—. "Fetishization", in E. Wright, 1992

—. *Volatile Bodies*, Indiana University Press, Bloomington, I.N., 1994

—. "Refiguring Lesbian Desire", in L. Doan, 1994

—. *Space, Time and Perversion*, Routledge, London, 1995

H. Hughes. *Cinema Italiano*, I.B. Tauris, London, 2011

L. Irigaray. *This Sex Which Is Not One*, tr. C. Porter & C. Burke, Cornell University Press, New York, 1977

—. *Speculum of the Other Woman*, tr. G.C. Gill, Cornell University Press, New York, 1985

—. *Sexes et parentés*, Minuit, Paris, 1987

—. *The Irigaray Reader,* ed. M. Whitford, Blackwell, Oxford, 1991

S. Jaworzy, ed. *Shock: The Essential Guide to Exploitation Cinema*, Titan Books, London, 1996

C.G. Jung. *Memories, Dreams, Reflections*, Collins, London, 1967

C. Kessler. "How You Look at It: The Beastly Art of Walerian Borowczyk", in *Video Watchdog*, Special Edition, 1

—. *Cinema Papers*, 128, 129

Julia Kristeva. *About Chinese Women*, tr. A. Barrows, Boyars, London, 1977

—. *Powers of Horror: An Essay On Abjection*, tr. L.S. Roudiez, Columbia University Press, New York, 1982

—. *The Kristeva Reader*, ed. Toril Moi, Blackwell, Oxford, 1986

—. *Tales of Love*, tr. L.S. Roudiez, Columbia University Press, New York, 1987

—. *Black Sun: Depression and Melancholy,* tr. L.S. Roudiez, Columbia University Press, New York, 1989

A. Kuhn. *Women's Pictures: Feminism and the Cinema*, Routledge & Kegan Paul, London, 1982

—. *Cinema, Censorship and Sexuality, 1909-1925*, Routledge, London, 1988

—. ed. *Alien Zone: Cultural Theory and Contemporary Science Fiction*, Verso, London, 1990

—. ed. *Alien Zone 2*, Verso, London, 1999

K. Kuc, ed. *Boro, L'Ile d'Amour*, Berghahn, 2015

S. Laroque-Texier. *Lecture de Mandiargues*, L'Harmattan, Paris, 2005

C. Leroy. *Le mythe de la passante de Baudelaire à Mandiargues*, P.U.F., Paris, 1999

A. Mallard & S. Pieyre de Mandiargues, *André Pieyre de Mandiargues*, Gallimard, 2009

Elaine Marks & Isabelle de Courtivron, eds. *New French Feminisms: an Anthology,* Harvester Wheatsheaf, 1981

F. Martellucci. *L'occhio libro: Studio sul linguaggio dell'immagine nella poesia di André Pieyre de Mandiargues*, Bulzoni, Rome, 1995

Tom Milne. "Les Héroïnes du mal (Three Immoral Women)", *Monthly Film Bulletin*, July, 1981

Toril Moi. *Sexual/ Textual Politics: Feminist Literary*

Theory, Routledge, London, 1988

—. ed. *French Feminist Thought*, Blackwell, Oxford, 1988

S. Murray. "Walerian Borowczyk's Heroines of Desire", *Senses of Cinema*, July, 2005

K. Newman. *Nightmare Movies*, Harmony, New York, N.Y., 1988

—. & J. Marriott. *Horror! The Definitive Companion To the Most Terrifying Movies Ever Made*, Carlton Books, London, 2013

I. & P. Opie. *The Classic Fairy Tales*, Paladin, 1980

P.P. Pasolini. *Pasolini On Pasolini*, ed. Oswald Stack, Thames & Hudson, London, 1969

F. Patriarca & S. Pieyre de Mandiargues, *L'appartement*, Filigranes Éditions, 2004

J. Pierre. *Le Belvédère Mandiargues*, Biron, Paris, 1990

M. Praz. *The Romantic Agony,* tr. Davidson, Oxford University Press, Oxford, 1933

E.D. Pribram, ed. *Female Spectators: Looking At Film and TV*, Verso, London, 1988

M. Richardson. *Surrealism and Cinema*, Berg, New York, N.Y., 2006

D. Schaefer & L. Salvato, eds. *Masters of Light*, University of California Press,Berkeley, CA, 1984

C. Seelinger. *Walerian Borowczyks Literarische Objekte der Begierde*, Büchner, 2019

S. Stétié. *Mandiargues*, Seghers, Paris, 1978

B. Thomas. *Disney's Art of Animation From Mickey Mouse To Beauty and the Beast*, Hyperion, New York, N.Y., 1991

D. Thomson. "That Hairy Monster" [on Walerian Borowczyk's *The Beast*], *Sight & Sound*, June, 2001

C. Tohill & P. Tombs. *Immoral Tales: Sex and Horror Cinema in Europe 1956-1984*, Titan Books, London, 1995

P. Verlaine. *Selected Poems*, tr. J. Richardson, Penguin, London, 1974

Walerian Borowczyk di Valerio Caprara, La Nuova Italia, Florence, 1981

M. Warner. *From the Beast To the Blonde: On Fairy Tales and Their Tellers*, Vintage, London, 1995

Linda Watson. *20th Century Fashion*, Carlton, London, 2003

J. White. "Blu-ray Review: *Immoral Tales*", the Last

Picture Show, 2014

Elizabeth Wright, ed. *Feminism and Psychoanalysis: A Critical Dictionary*, Blackwell, Oxford, 1992

J. Zipes. *Fairy Tales and the Art of Subversion: The Classical Genre for Children and the Process of Civilization*, Heinemann, London, 1983

—. *Trials and Tribulations of Little Red Riding Hood: Versions of the Tale in Socio-Cultural Context*, Heinemann, London, 1983

—. *Don't Bet On the Prince: Contemporary Feminist Fairy Tales in North America and England*, Methuen, New York, N.Y., 1986

—. *The Brothers Grimm: From Enchanted Forests To the Modern World*, Routledge, New York, N.Y., 1989

—. ed. *The Oxford Companion To Fairy Tales*, Oxford University Press, 2000

—. *Sticks and Stones: The Troublesome Success of Children's Literature from Slovenly Peter To Harry Potter*, Routledge,, London, 2002

—. *The Enchanted Screen: The Unknown History of Fairy-tale Films*, Routledge, New York, N.Y., 2011

—. *The Irresistible Fairy Tale*, Prince University Press, Princeton, N.J., 2012

WEBSITES

Walerian Borowczyk: walerianborowczyk.com
Ubuweb: ubu.com
Animation World Network: awm.com/ gallery/boro/info
Marina Pierro: www.marinapierro.com
Bernard Parmegiani: bernard-parmegiani.fr

JEREMY ROBINSON has published poetry, fiction, and studies of J.R.R. Tolkien, Samuel Beckett, Thomas Hardy, André Gide and D.H. Lawrence. Robinson has edited poetry books by Novalis, Ursula Le Guin, Friedrich Hölderlin, Francesco Petrarch, Dante Alighieri, Arseny Tarkovsky, and Rainer Maria Rilke.

Books on film and animation include: *The Akira Book* • *The Art of Katsuhiro Otomo* • *The Art of Masamune Shirow* • *The Ghost In the Shell Book* • *Fullmetal Alchemist* • *Cowboy Bebop: The Anime and Movie* • *The Cinema of Hayao Miyazaki* • *Hayao Miyazaki: Pocket Guide* • *Princess Mononoke: Pocket Movie Guide* • *Spirited Away: Pocket Movie Guide* • *Blade Runner and the Cinema of Philip K. Dick* • *Blade Runner: Pocket Movie Guide* • *The Cinema of Donald Cammell* • *Performance: Donald Cammell: Nic Roeg: Pocket Movie Guide* • *Pasolini: Il Cinema di Poesia/ The Cinema of Poetry* • *Salo: Pocket Movie Guide* • *The Trilogy of Life Movies: Pocket Movie Guide* • *The Gospel According To Matthew: Pocket Movie Guide* • *The Ecstatic Cinema of Tony Ching Siu-tung* • *Tsui Hark: The Dragon Master of Chinese Cinema* • *The Swordsman: Pocket Movie Guide* • *A Chinese Ghost Story: Pocket Movie Guide* • *Ken Russell: England's Great Visionary Film Director and Music Lover* • *Tommy: Ken Russell: The Who: Pocket Movie Guide* • *Women In Love: Ken Russell: D.H. Lawrence: Pocket Movie Guide* • *The Devils: Ken Russell: Pocket Movie Guide* • *Walerian Borowczyk: Cinema of Erotic Dreams* • *The Beast: Pocket Movie Guide* • *The Lord of the Rings Movies* • *The Fellowship of the Ring: Pocket Movie Guide* • *The Two Towers: Pocket Movie Guide* • *The Return of the King: Pocket Movie Guide* • *Jean-Luc Godard: The Passion of Cinema* • *The Sacred Cinema of Andrei Tarkovsky* • *Andrei Tarkovsky: Pocket Guide.*

'It's amazing for me to see my work treated with such passion and respect. There is nothing resembling it in the U.S. in relation to my work.'
(Andrea Dworkin)

'This model monograph – it is an exemplary job, and I'm very proud that he has accorded me a couple of mentions… The subject matter of his book is beautifully organised and dead on beam.'
(Lawrence Durrell, on *The Light Eternal: A Study of J.M.W. Turner*)

'Jeremy Robinson's poetry is certainly jammed with ideas, and I find it very interesting for that reason. It's certainly a strong imprint of his personality.'
(Colin Wilson)

'*Sex-Magic-Poetry-Cornwall* is a very rich essay... It is a very good piece… vastly stimulating and insightful.'
(Peter Redgrove)

In the Dim Void

Samuel Beckett's Late Trilogy:
Company, Ill Seen, Ill Said and *Worstward Ho*

by Gregory Johns

This book discusses the luminous beauty and dense, rigorous poetry of Samuel Beckett's late works, *Company, Ill Seen, Ill Said* and *Worstward Ho*. Gregory Johns looks back over Beckett's long writing career, charting the development from the *Molloy-Malone Dies-Unnamable* trilogy through the 'fizzles' of the 1960s to the elegiac lyricism of the *Company* series. Johns compares the trilogy with late plays such as *Ghosts, Footfalls* and *Rockaby*.

Bibliography, notes. Illustrated. 120pp
ISBN 9781861712974 Pbk and ISBN 9781861712608 Hbk
9781861713407 E-book

ARTS, PAINTING, SCULPTURE

web: www.crmoon.com • e-mail: cresmopub@yahoo.co.uk

The Art of Andy Goldsworthy
Andy Goldsworthy: Touching Nature
Andy Goldsworthy in Close-Up
Andy Goldsworthy: Pocket Guide
Andy Goldsworthy In America
Land Art: A Complete Guide
The Art of Richard Long
Richard Long: Pocket Guide
Land Art In Great Britain
Land Art in Close-Up
Land Art In the U.S.A.
Land Art: Pocket Guide
Installation Art in Close-Up
Minimal Art and Artists In the 1960s and After
Colourfield Painting
Land Art DVD, TV documentary
Andy Goldsworthy DVD, TV documentary
The Erotic Object: Sexuality in Sculpture From Prehistory to the Present Day
Sex in Art: Pornography and Pleasure in Painting and Sculpture
Postwar Art
Sacred Gardens: The Garden in Myth, Religion and Art
Glorification: Religious Abstraction in Renaissance and 20th Century Art
Early Netherlandish Painting
Jasper Johns
Brice MardenLeonardo da Vinci
Piero della Francesca
Giovanni Bellini
Fra Angelico: Art and Religion in the Renaissance
Mark Rothko: The Art of Transcendence
Frank Stella: American Abstract Artist
Alison Wilding: The Embrace of Sculpture
Vincent van Gogh: Visionary Landscapes
Eric Gill: Nuptials of God
Constantin Brancusi: Sculpting the Essence of Things
Max Beckmann
Gustave Moreau
Caravaggio
Egon Schiele: Sex and Death In Purple Stockings
Delizioso Fotografico Fervore: Works In Process I
Sacro Cuore: Works In Process 2
The Light Eternal: J.M.W. Turner
The Madonna Glorified: Karen Arthurs

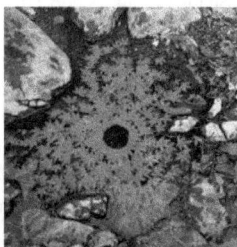

LITERATURE

J.R.R. Tolkien: The Books, The Films, The Whole Cultural Phenomenon
J.R.R. Tolkien: Pocket Guide
Beauties, Beasts and Enchantment: Classic French Fairy Tales
Tolkien's Heroic Quest
Brothers Grimm: German Popular Stories
Sexing Hardy: Thomas Hardy and Feminism
Thomas Hardy's *Tess of the d'Urbervilles*
Thomas Hardy's *Jude the Obscure*
Thomas Hardy: The Tragic Novels
Love and Tragedy: Thomas Hardy
The Poetry of Landscape in Hardy
Wessex Revisited: Thomas Hardy and John Cowper Powys
Wolfgang Iser: Essays and Interviews
Petrarch, Dante and the Troubadours
Maurice Sendak and the Art of Children's Book Illustration
Andrea Dworkin
Cixous, Irigaray, Kristeva: The *Jouissance* of French Feminism
Julia Kristeva: Art, Love, Melancholy, Philosophy, Semiotics and Psychoanalysis
Hélene Cixous I Love You: The *Jouissance* of Writing
Luce Irigaray: Lips, Kissing, and the Politics of Sexual Difference
Peter Redgrove: Here Comes the Flood
Peter Redgrove: Sex-Magic-Poetry-Cornwall
Lawrence Durrell: Between Love and Death, East and West
Love, Culture & Poetry: Lawrence Durrell
Cavafy: Anatomy of a Soul
German Romantic Poetry: Goethe, Novalis, Heine, Hölderlin
Novalis: *Hymns To the Night*
Feminism and Shakespeare
Shakespeare: *The Sonnets*
Shakespeare: Love, Poetry & Magic
The Passion of D.H. Lawrence
D.H. Lawrence: Symbolic Landscapes
D.H. Lawrence: Infinite Sensual Violence
The Ecstasies of John Cowper Powys
Sensualism and Mythology: The Wessex Novels of John Cowper Powys
Amorous Life: John Cowper Powys (H.W. Fawkner)
Postmodern Powys: New Essays on John Cowper Powys (Joe Boulter)
Rethinking Powys: Critical Essays on John Cowper Powys
Paul Bowles & Bernardo Bertolucci
Rainer Maria Rilke
Joseph Conrad: *Heart of Darkness*
In the Dim Void: Samuel Beckett
Samuel Beckett Goes into the Silence
André Gide: Fiction and Fervour
Jackie Collins and the Blockbuster Novel
Blinded By Her Light: The Love-Poetry of Robert Graves

POETRY

Ursula Le Guin: *Walking In Cornwall*
Peter Redgrove: Here Comes The Flood
Peter Redgrove: Sex-Magic-Poetry-Cornwall
Dante: Selections From the *Vita Nuova*
Petrarch, Dante and the Troubadours
William Shakespeare: *The Sonnets*
William Shakespeare: Complete Poems
Blinded By Her Light: The Love-Poetry of Robert Graves
Emily Dickinson: Selected Poems
Emily Brontë: Poems
Thomas Hardy: Selected Poems
Percy Bysshe Shelley: Poems
John Keats: Selected Poems
John Keats: Poems of 1820
D.H. Lawrence: Selected Poems
Edmund Spenser: Poems
Edmund Spenser: *Amoretti*
John Donne: Poems
Henry Vaughan: Poems
Sir Thomas Wyatt: Poems
Robert Herrick: Selected Poems
Rilke: Space, Essence and Angels in the Poetry of Rainer Maria Rilke
Rainer Maria Rilke: Selected Poems
Friedrich Hölderlin: Selected Poems
Arseny Tarkovsky: Selected Poems
Paul Verlaine: Selected Poems
Novalis: *Hymns To the Night*
Arthur Rimbaud: Selected Poems
Arthur Rimbaud: *A Season in Hell*
Arthur Rimbaud and the Magic of Poetry
D.J. Enright: By-Blows
Jeremy Reed: *Brigitte's Blue Heart*
Jeremy Reed: *Claudia Schiffer's Red Shoes*
Gorgeous Little Orpheus
Radiance: New Poems
Crescent Moon Book of Nature Poetry
Crescent Moon Book of Love Poetry
Crescent Moon Book of Mystical Poetry
Crescent Moon Book of Elizabethan Love Poetry
Crescent Moon Book of Metaphysical Poetry
Crescent Moon Book of Romantic Poetry
Pagan America: New American Poetry

MEDIA, CINEMA, FEMINISM and CULTURAL STUDIES

J.R.R. Tolkien: The Books, The Films, The Whole Cultural Phenomenon
J.R.R. Tolkien: Pocket Guide
The *Lord of the Rings* Movies: Pocket Guide
The Ghost Dance: The Origins of Religion
The Cinema of Hayao Miyazaki
Hayao Miyazaki: *Princess Mononoke*: Pocket Movie Guide
Hayao Miyazaki: *Spirited Away*: Pocket Movie Guide
The Peyote Cult
HomeGround: The Kate Bush Anthology
Tim Burton : Hallowe'en For Hollywood
Ken Russell
Cixous, Irigaray, Kristeva: The *Jouissance* of French Feminism
Julia Kristeva: Art, Love, Melancholy, Philosophy, Semiotics and Psychoanalysis
Luce Irigaray: Lips, Kissing, and the Politics of Sexual Difference
Hélène Cixous I Love You: The *Jouissance* of Writing
Andrea Dworkin
'Cosmo Woman': The World of Women's Magazines
Women in Pop Music
Discovering the Goddess (Geoffrey Ashe)
The Poetry of Cinema
The Sacred Cinema of Andrei Tarkovsky
Andrei Tarkovsky: Pocket Guide
Andrei Tarkovsky: *Mirror*: Pocket Movie Guide
Walerian Borowczyk: Cinema of Erotic Dreams
Jean-Luc Godard: The Passion of Cinema
Jean-Luc Godard: Pocket Guide
John Hughes and Eighties Cinema
Ferris Buller's Day Off: Pocket Movie Guide
The Cinema of Richard Linklater
Liv Tyler: Star In Ascendance
Blade Runner and the Films of Philip K. Dick
Paul Bowles and Bernardo Bertolucci
Media Hell: Radio, TV and the Press
Detonation Britain: Nuclear War in the UK
Feminism and Shakespeare
Wild Zones: Pornography, Art and Feminism
Sex in Art: Pornography and Pleasure in Painting and Sculpture
Sexing Hardy: Thomas Hardy and Feminism

The Light Eternal *is a model monograph, an exemplary job. The subject matter of the book is
beautifully organised and dead on beam.* (Lawrence Durrell)
It is amazing for me to see my work treated with such passion and respect. (Andrea Dworkin)
Sex-Magic-Poetry-Cornwall *is a very rich essay... It is like a brightly-lighted box.* (Peter Redgrove

CRESCENT MOON PUBLISHING P.O. Box 1312, Maidstone, Kent, ME14 5XU, Great Britai
0044-1622-729593 cresmopub@yahoo.co.uk www.crmoon.com